To Daniel,

With best wishes,

Leslie W. Hepple

26 July 1977

A HISTORY OF NORTHUMBERLAND
AND NEWCASTLE UPON TYNE

Bamburgh Castle. Ida the Angle established his base here in about 547 and it became the Northumbrian capital. Robert de Mowbray, Earl of Northumberland, was besieged here in 1095 by William Rufus, and the Castle was twice besieged during the Wars of the Roses. In 1826 two parliamentary candidates fought a duel on these sands in front of the Castle.

THE DARWEN COUNTY HISTORY SERIES

A History of Northumberland and Newcastle Upon Tyne

LESLIE W. HEPPLE

Drawings by CAROLYN LOCKWOOD

PHILLIMORE

First published 1976
by
PHILLIMORE & CO., LTD.,
London and Chichester

Head Office: Shopwyke Hall
Chichester, Sussex, England

ISBN 0 85033 245 1

Printed in England by
UNWIN BROTHERS, LTD.,
at The Gresham Press, Old Woking, Surrey

Contents

Late 14th-century silver seal and chain of Henry de Burradon (in Coquetdale), found in a peat-bog in North Tynedale

Maps and Plans

TO MY MOTHER AND FATHER

13th-century bronze decorative water-ewer found beside the South Tyne

List of Illustrations

Acknowledgements

The author wishes to thank the following for permission to use their photographs: Philipson Studios, Newcastle (frontispiece and nos. 4 and 15); Mr. G. Jobey, University of Newcastle Upon Tyne (no. 1); Mrs. U. M. Chatfield (no. 20); The Committee for Aerial Photography, Cambridge University (photographs by Professor J. K. St. Joseph) (nos. 2, 5, 14); The University of Newcastle Upon Tyne (photographs by Professor N. McCord) (nos. 3, 8, 17, 33); *Country Life* (no. 6); The Shipley Art Gallery, Gateshead (Tyne and Wear County Museums Service) (no. 27); The Public Record Office and the Society of Antiquaries of Newcastle Upon Tyne (no. 13) (Crown copyright); The Society of Antiquaries of Newcastle Upon Tyne (nos. 10, 16); Mr. R. W. Hepple (no. 34).

Maps 8 and 9 are reproduced by kind permission of Dr. J. Langton (University of Liverpool), and the Editor, *Transactions of the Institute of British Geographers.*

Preface

Northumberland has been well served by its historians. As early as the 17th century Roger North found the people around Hexham 'great antiquarians within their own bounds', and ever since John Horsley the Morpeth Presbyterian minister wrote his *Britannia* in the 1720s Roman studies have been keenly pursued in the county. The Society of Antiquaries of Newcastle, founded in 1813, is the oldest such society outside London, and the multi-volume *History* by John Hodgson and later the 15 volumes by the County History Committee put the county, in R. G. Collingwood's words, 'in a class of its own'.

There is, however, no modern short history of Northumberland for the general reader or for the local historian who wants a framework within which to put his detailed enquiries. Like other volumes in this series, this book tries to present such an introductory account. Local and regional history is still a fast developing field and within the limits of a short study this book tries to give an up-to-date account including recent interpretations and research. Local history today is less about battles and the political chess of barons than it used to be, and more about social and economic changes, and much of our understanding of medieval society, to take only one example, is very recent. Even the well-tilled area of Roman studies remains fresh and controversial. A history of this length must be highly selective, and the bibliography provides a guide to further reading and reference sources.

No history of Northumberland could be complete without including Newcastle Upon Tyne. Although Newcastle has been a separate administrative county since 1400, it has been the economic and political centre of Northumberland since medieval times. Within Newcastle itself the area of the royal Castle remained part of Northumberland. Throughout the book the pre-1974 boundaries of Northumberland and Newcastle have been used. The re-drawing of the boundaries, creating the new Tyne and Wear County, is too recent to have had much impact, and it is the traditional county units that have been the framework for many centuries of history.

Although it is impossible to trace ordinary families through the centuries of Northumberland history, some landowning families have been remarkably tenacious over the years. As a minor thread running through some of the chapters, I have used the Craster family of Craster near Embleton as illustrations. There were Crasters at Craster in 1166 and in 1966. They were at Agincourt, in the Civil War, and on the 18th-century Grand Tour. They claimed serfs in the 13th century and improved their farms in the 18th, fought duels and became Newcastle merchants. The final chapter of the book also brings together some of the themes by looking in detail at one very local landscape and its history: Guyzance and Acklington on the lower Coquet.

Line illustrations are amongst the delights of older books on Northumberland, and I am most grateful to Carolyn Lockwood for her numerous charming drawings for this book. It is also a pleasure to thank Simon Godden of the Department of Geography, University of Bristol, who drew most of the maps, and Tony Philpott of the same Department, who helped considerably with the photographic work. My parents first sparked my interest in local history. This book is dedicated to them with affection and gratitude. My greatest debt is to my wife Suzanne, who has encouraged and assisted me with the book right through from the first stages to the final typing and indexing.

Tyne Bridge, Newcastle

I The Landscape

Yeavering Bell

Northumberland is England's northernmost county, and forms the major part of the border with Scotland. It was the last of the English counties to receive its modern form, for not until 1844 were the lands of North Durham (Norhamshire, Islandshire and Bedlingtonshire) incorporated into the administrative county. It was the fifth largest county, until the local government changes of 1974 detached its south-east fringe to form part of the new Tyne and Wear county. Yet the region has an historical unity that will not easily be destroyed by administrative changes. It has a varied landscape of shipyards and wooded river valleys, pit villages and windy moorlands. The magnificent coastline alternates between long, sandy beaches and rocky headlands. The boundaries of the county are well defined: the Tyne and Pennine foothills in the south, the Cheviots and border moorlands in the north-west, and the winding Tweed in the north. But although the boundaries are logical divides, and Northumberland is a clearer physical unit than most English counties, the historian should not make too much of them. If Anglo-Saxon and medieval history had gone differently in the north, as it might well have, the northern border could have been the Firth of Forth, or the Tyne the southern boundary of Scotland. The unity of Northumberland lies in the common experience of how history did go.

The highest ground is formed by the Cheviot Hills. The Cheviot itself, at 2,676 feet, is visible on a clear day from Newcastle, and in earlier times was an aid to navigation at sea. In the 17th century William Gray called it 'a landmark for seamen that comes out of the east parts from Danzicke, through the Baltick seas, and from the King of Denmark's countrey; it being the first land that mariners make for the coast of England'. The Cheviot granite is the stump of an ancient volcano, with rounded scenery of peat-bog and heather. Around it the ring of lavas support bracken and bent. This upland country must always have been largely open, a land of the sheep and the falcon, but not exclusively so, for in about 1538 Leland, the antiquary, wrote of 'the great wood of Cheviot' which was 'spoyled now and crokyd old trees and scrubs remayne'.

The Northumbrian dales, moors and scarplands lie between the Cheviot Hills and the lowlands of the coast and Tyne. Around the Cheviot massif, where the volcanic lavas give way to the easily-eroded

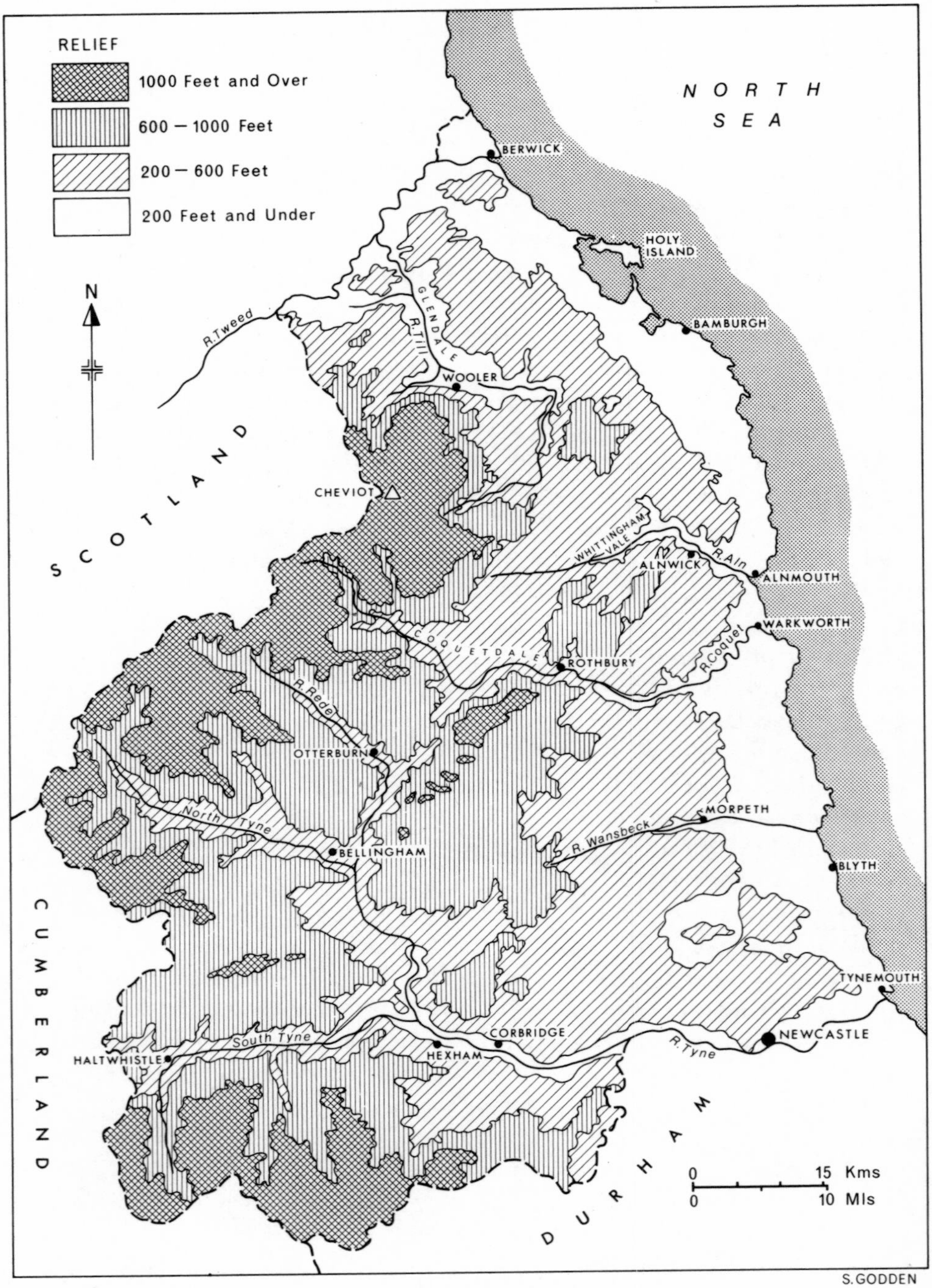

RELIEF
1000 Feet and Over
600 — 1000 Feet
200 — 600 Feet
200 Feet and Under
N
NORTH SEA
SCOTLAND
CUMBERLAND
DURHAM
BERWICK
HOLY ISLAND
BAMBURGH
R.Tweed
R.Till
GLENDALE
WOOLER
CHEVIOT
WHITTINGHAM VALE
R.Aln
ALNWICK
ALNMOUTH
WARKWORTH
COQUETDALE
ROTHBURY
R.Coquet
R.Rede
OTTERBURN
North Tyne
BELLINGHAM
R. Wansbeck
MORPETH
BLYTH
TYNEMOUTH
NEWCASTLE
R.Tyne
CORBRIDGE
HEXHAM
South Tyne
HALTWHISTLE
0 15 Kms
0 10 Mls
S.GODDEN

1. Northumberland: Relief

shales of the Cementstones, the scenery abruptly changes (at places like Alwinton and Alnham) to the broad, low-lying vales of the Coquet, Aln, Breamish and Till rivers, and a landscape of farms, hedges and fields. These open valleys were settled early, and in medieval surveys they contained many of the richest villages in Northumberland, though the Till valley, littered with glacial sands and moraines, was (and still is) susceptible to flooding by the melting snows and summer rains. The Coquet is probably the finest valley (though many would argue for Whittingham Vale), and also a renowned trout-fishing river. Between these vales and the lowland plain are the resistant Fell Sandstones that form the scarplands of the Kyloe Hills, Ros Castle, and the Chillingham ridge, Corby Crags, the Simonsides and Harbottle Crag. These rocks make good building stones, and have been the main stone used for Northumbrian castles, churches and country-houses since Roman times. The scarps face in towards the Cheviots, and their summits provide some of the finest views in all Northumberland, though the fells themselves have thin, sandy soils and have been of little agricultural value.

In the south-west of the county the Cementstones and Sandstones are squeezed into a narrow belt along the border line, and the moorland scenery is made of the Carboniferous limestone that elsewhere lies under the coastal plain. Here the moors stretch to the horizon, broken only by occasional outcrops of sandstones, such as the Wannies, and the great volcanic dyke known as the Whin Sill that cuts through the Northumberland landscape from the south-west to the sea-coast and the Farnes, with its most dramatic sections on the Roman Wall near Housesteads and on the coast at Dunstanburgh and Bamburgh. The valleys of the North Tyne and Rede cut through the moorlands, but they are narrow and much more cut off from the rest of Northumberland than the broad vales of the Coquet, Till and Aln. This relative isolation of the North Tyne and Rede encouraged the development of a very wild and distinctive border society in the late medieval period.

The Northumberland lowlands stretch in a crescent around these moors and hills, from the border waters of the Tweed in the north, down the coast to Tynemouth and west along the Tyne valley. Here the solid rocks are generally overlain by glacial tills of clay and sand that give potentially good farming country, though south of the Coquet the clays of the coastal plain are heavy. The south-east corner is the economic heart of modern Northumberland. It forms an industrial triangle from Newcastle (which established its dominance over the economic life of the county in medieval times and has retained it ever since) down the Tyne to Tynemouth, then up the coast to Amble. Small coal seams occur near the surface in many parts of

Holy Island Castle

Collingwood Monument, Tynemouth

Northumberland, but the thick, rich seams that were the basis of the county's industrial growth (and many of its 20th-century problems) lay under the boulder clays of south-east Northumberland.

The value of landscapes and regions alters with changing technology and circumstance, and before the expansion of coal-mining the south-east of the county was not a prosperous area, except for the immediate vicinity of Newcastle itself. The heavy clay soils were difficult for farming, and many areas only became useful after the introduction of underfield tile-draining in the 1840s and 1850s. The coastal plain north of the Coquet, with sandier, more loamy soils, was the prosperous, productive region of Anglian and medieval Northumberland. Similarly, the usefulness of the coastline itself has changed. The coast from Tyne to Tweed has few large harbours, and as early as the 1540s the King's fleet had to anchor in the shallow water of Skate Road off Holy Island, yet in medieval and earlier times the tiny ships could use many of the bays and small harbours on the coast. Even Dunstanburgh Castle had its harbour, now a muddy stretch in front of the castle, cut off from the sea by shingle, where in 1514 the warships of Henry VIII took refuge.

Attitudes to the landscape have also changed, and our present appreciation of Northumberland's moorland hills and coastal scenery was not always shared in the past. An 18th-century Rector of Elsdon, the Rev. Dodgson, was completely unimpressed by the moors of the Middle Marches, and when Vanbrugh built Seaton Delaval Hall in the 1720s he ignored the potential sea views the Hall could have had. By 1750 Tynemouth's beaches and coves were already popular for the sea-air and bathing, but in about 1200 a monk from St. Albans thought very differently of the place: 'Thick sea-frets roll in, wrapping everything in gloom. Dim eyes, hoarse voices, sore throats are the consequence'. He continued: 'In the spring the sea-air blights the blossoms of the stunted fruit trees, so that you will think yourself lucky to find a wizened apple, though it will set your teeth on edge should you try to eat it. See to it, dear brother, that you do not come to so comfortless a place'. We ought, however, to remember the unglazed windows, bare stone floors and lack of good heating in medieval Tynemouth.

The present appearance of the Northumberland landscape is very largely man-made. The natural landscape was much more wooded than today, especially on the coastal plain and in the river valleys, though the analysis of pollen grains preserved in the peat-bogs of moorland Northumberland north of the Roman Wall has shown that many of these areas were also wooded, until forest clearance in Iron Age and Anglo-Saxon times. Clearing the woodland encouraged soil

1. Bronze Age burial cist at Shipley near Alnwick.

2. Yeavering Bell, the largest Iron Age hillfort in the county. The Anglian palace of *Ad Gefrin* was in the Glen valley to the north.

3. Iron Age and Romano-British settlement at Hartburn, during excavation in 1971.

4. The Roman Wall, looking east near Housesteads.

erosion, and river silting resulted, aided by man-made obstacles like weirs and fish-traps, which became a major problem on the medieval Tyne. The original landscape left after glaciation was very marshy and wet. Many place-names record this original state (such as Morwick, farm by the swamp), and numerous mires and lakes have been drained, the large Prestwick Carr near Ponteland as late as 1860.

There have also been natural changes in the environment. The river Coquet used to turn abruptly north at Amble before entering the sea, until in 1765 it cut the present mouth and left a long neck of dunes on the north side of the river as an isolated part of Amble township. In 1806 a storm caused a similar change at Alnmouth, when the river Aln shifted its mouth northward and cut the old church off from the village. The Northumbrian climate has been unstable. After the Norman Conquest the climate improved, with warmer weather and longer growing seasons, to an optimum about 1150 to 1300. Cultivation was possible higher up the hills than it is today. Yet after 1300 the climate deteriorated and became colder and wetter. The margins of arable farming contracted downhill, and a study on the Lammermuir Hills, north of the border, has estimated that the upper limit of cultivation fell by 460 feet. This decline was gradual, though the appalling weather of 1315–17 provides a good starting date. After 1550 there was a further decline into what is known throughout Europe as the 'Little Ice Age', and only after 1700 did the climate improve. One must therefore sympathise with the Tudor officials sent north from London who complained about the Northumbrian weather. The poor Duke of Norfolk, who suffered from chronic diarrhoea, begged the King in October 1542 not to make him winter in the cold of Alnwick 'for assuredly I know if I should tarry in these parties it should cost me my life'. In December 1595 Lord Willoughby, governor of Berwick, wrote: 'if I were further from the tempestuousness of Cheviot Hills and were once retired from this accursed country, whence the sun is so removed, I would not change my homliest hermitage for the highest palace'. Six months later he died of a great cold and fever. Fortunately, the present Northumbrian climate is considerably pleasanter.

High and Low Lights, North Shields

II Prehistoric Northumberland

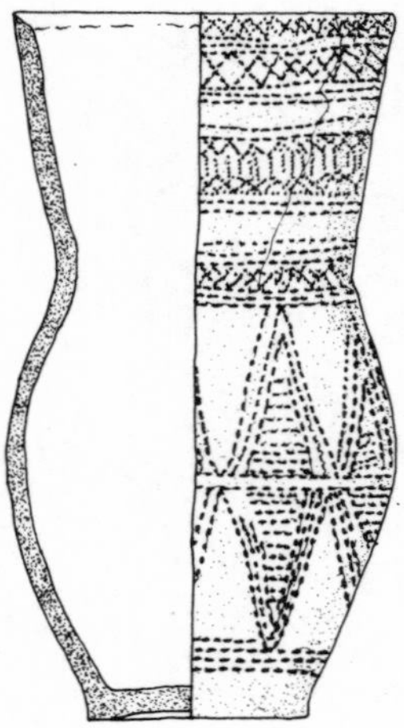

Beaker from Shipley cist

The earliest settlers in Northumberland, during the Middle Stone Age of 5000–3000 B.C., were few in number and have left only a few traces of pigmy flints around Budle Bay near Bamburgh, and in the Tweed Valley. Rather more evidence comes from the succeeding Neolithic period, in the form of stone axes from 'factories' such as those at Langdale in the Lake District, and a few barrows and cairns, but it is a meagre record compared with that found in other parts of Britain, or with later periods in Northumberland. Much more extensive evidence comes after the Beaker invasions that began about 1800 B.C.

The Beaker invaders arrived by sea from the continent, though the Northumbrian settlement may be an offshoot of groups further south. Along the Northumbrian coast they penetrated up the river valleys of the Tyne, Coquet and Aln, and landed in the bays north of the Coquet, but they avoided the densely wooded, heavy clays of south-east Northumberland, and their main settlement was north of the Aln, where higher ground and lighter soils gave more accessible and less wooded country close to the coast. We know very little of the settlements of these invaders, but a good deal about their funeral practices. Their custom was inhumation, the placing of the body in a stone cist in the ground, usually together with their typical beaker-pottery from which they get their name. These cists were sometimes topped by a small barrow or cairn. The technique of radio-carbon assay of organic deposits found in archaeological sites is now allowing more precise dating for such burials. Excavation of a large cairn at Chatton Sandyford, on the moors between Chillingham and North Charlton, revealed beaker burials, the first of which was dated to about 1670 B.C. Beaker cists are quite dense on the ground, and have frequently been found in farming. An example is one that was turned up during ploughing at Shipley near Alnwick in 1958. The cist contained the crouched skeleton of a female, aged 30–40 at death, and of the brachycephalic or broad, round-skulled type characteristic of the Beaker people, together with the usual beaker (Plate 1). The skeleton shows the wound on her arm that may have caused her death. After opening and excavation the cists usually get filled with earth, but one example is visible on the north-east slopes of Lordenshaws Hill, south of

Rothbury. This is a good locality for seeing remains from all of the Bronze Age, Iron Age, Romano-British, and medieval periods.

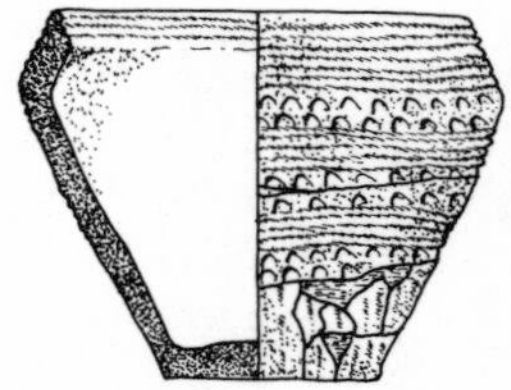

Food Vessel from Lilburn

The Beaker people mixed with the local population, and their absorption into the local populace is marked by a change in the type of pottery found: a 'Food Vessel' emerges as an amalgam of the Neolithic ware and the Beaker tradition. There was clearly an expansion of population, with settlement in areas of Tynedale previously largely uninhabited. In general the same burial practices continued. At a later date, probably about 1000 B.C., burial gave way to cremation, and in place of inhumations one finds cinerary urns. However, cremation did occur in Beaker times, as is instanced by the excavation of a barrow at Howick Heugh near Craster in 1972, which revealed a cremation dated from the charcoal of the funeral pyre to about 1440 B.C.

At probably about the same time as the Beaker invasions, a much weaker influx of Neolithic groups came from the west and north. It is likely that these groups created the few megalithic monuments to be found in the county, such as the stone-circles at Duddo, Threestoneburn in the Cheviots, and the Goatstones and Three Kings in south-west Northumberland. They belong to a number of different traditions, but H. A. W. Burl's comment that the Goatstones and Three Kings were 'shrivelled survivors of the Neolithic tradition of megalithic burial' in a region not their own, is likely to be applicable to many of them. Also from this period are the strange 'cup-and-ring' designs of carved spirals, whorls and circles to be found on many rocks in the sandstone areas of Northumberland. These carvings, seemingly of religious significance in the way that Christians later carved a cross or fish, can be seen on Lordenshaws south of Rothbury and on the moors east of Wooler. Their contemporaneity with the Beaker period is indicated by their presence on the stones of burial cists, as on Fowberry Moor near Chatton.

The presence of bronze in the regional culture first occurs at about the same time as the Beaker people were mingling with the native population. At Allerwash, for example, near Newborough on the South Tyne, a bronze dagger was found in a cist that contained a mixture of Beaker and Neolithic burial traditions, suggesting a time when the main invasion thrust had waned. The flat blade, over 18 centimetres long, has three rivets at the butt where it was attached to a wooden handle. A similar dagger was found in a cist at Barrasford in North Tynedale, together with part of a brachycephalic skeleton, probably that of a man, aged 30–35 at death, about 5 feet 6 inches tall, and suffering from undernourishment on the evidence of the teeth and jawbone. The development of bronze

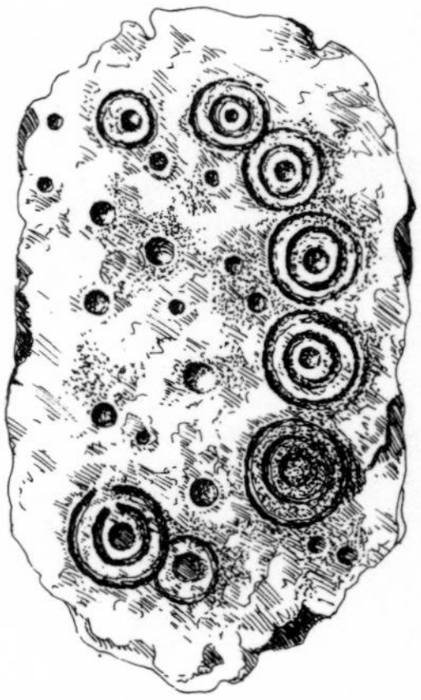

Cup-and-Ring carved rock

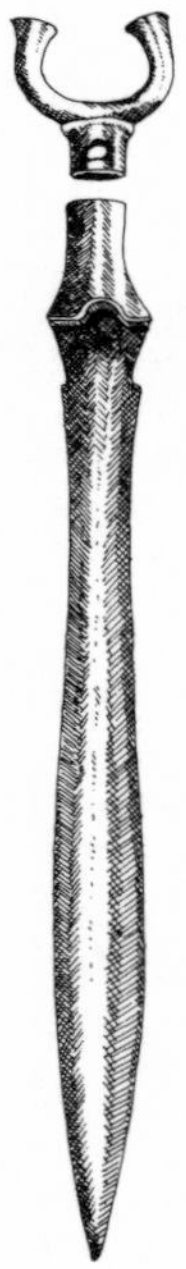

Whittingham sword

working was slow, but in terms of artistic styles seems to have been largely indigenous. The Bronze Age stayed late in this remote area, but there was a late flowering of some very fine bronze metalwork, best seen in the leaf-blade swords, such as the hoard found in 1847 near Thrunton Farm close to Whittingham, especially one sword with both a socketted blade and a socketted pommel.

The late Bronze Age in Northumberland merges almost imperceptibly into the so-called Iron Age of 500 B.C. onwards. Certainly there is little indication of iron-working in pre-Roman contexts. In one respect, however, Northumberland shows strong Iron Age features: the dominance of hillfort settlements. Unlike the earlier inhabitants, the local Late Bronze Age and Iron Age people have left little evidence of burial or cremation practices, but much evidence of their settlements. The Ordnance Survey maps of the upland parts of Northumberland have large numbers of 'camps' marked on them, but it is only in the last 20 years that their dating and sequence have been worked out, largely by G. Jobey. The earliest settlements are those revealed by aerial photography and excavation as timber-built compounds of wooden huts surrounded by wooden palisades. A site at High Knowes above Alnham in Whittingham Vale gave a radiocarbon date of 700 B.C. onwards. Other palisaded sites have been found underneath later settlements. The amount of wood required to build these villages serves as evidence of the more forested environment that then existed close to these now windswept sites.

Later in the Iron Age these palisaded settlements were succeeded by the defensive hillforts that are such a feature of the Northumbrian hills. The site at Huckhoe near Bolam lake suggests that stone defences replaced the palisade during the 6th century B.C., but both types clearly co-existed for a period: at Ingram hill a slight ditch with palisade is dated to about 285 B.C., whilst a more classic hillfort at Brough Law is dated to about the same time. Very fine examples of these forts can be seen at Lordenshaws, at Harehaugh, near Hepple on the Coquet, at Old Bewick, and at Ros Castle above Chillingham (a magnificent viewing-point for the north Northumberland landscape). In many cases the ditches and banks of stones and earth were subsequently multiplied, creating multivallate forts, as most of the above sites are. Typical sites are on the spurs of hills above river-valleys, but coastal headlands like Tynemouth and Dunstanburgh also had settlements. Within the defences, the huts were still wooden. Most sites were not much bigger than their palisaded predecessors, but the largest hillfort, at Yeavering Bell, has evidence of over 130 huts in it (Plate 2). These hillforts used frequently to be placed in a Roman context, but they are now firmly located in the pre-Roman centuries.

A new dimension to Iron Age settlement is beginning to emerge from aerial photography and excavation in lowland parts of the county. Large numbers of rectilinear enclosures are revealed by crop markings on aerial photographs of the coastal plain of south-east Northumberland. Most of these have been placed in a Roman context, but excavation has revealed some early pre-Roman Iron Age occupation. At Burradon, near Seghill, sherds of finger-impressed native pottery suggesting a 5th–6th-century B.C. date were found in a rectangular ditched enclosure containing evidence of round, timber-built huts. Further inland at Hartburn, excavation of a similar settlement also revealed pre-Roman Iron Age occupation. The wooden huts in these sites and in the hillforts had only limited lives, and both Hartburn and Burradon revealed good evidence of the sequence of replacement huts in the overlapping rings of post-holes (Plate 3).

This evidence is beginning to establish a pattern of Iron Age settlement in the inhospitable coastal clay plain, a development that is probably associated with the extensive Iron Age deforestation that is attested by the pollen diagrams for a number of sites in the north. Additional evidence of arable farming (in this largely pastoral region) on this clay soil comes from the presence of plough-marks found *below* the earliest Roman forts at Halton Chesters, Rudchester and Walker.

III Roman Northumberland

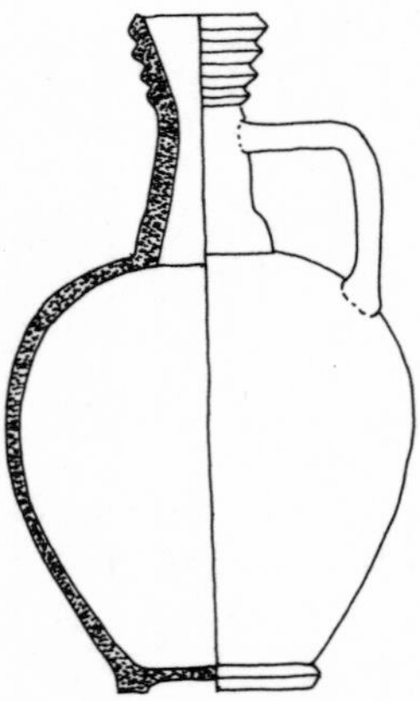

Coarse pottery flagon, Corbridge

The Roman occupation of Britain, which began with the invasion of Kent in 43 A.D., took over a generation to reach as far north as the Tyne. Then, under the governorship of Agricola, the Romans advanced into the foothills of the Scottish highlands in the early 'eighties. This campaign brought the Tyne-Tweed region under Roman control, and the area remained on the frontier of the Roman empire for the next 300 years. The forward line around the Highlands, with forts at Inchtuthil and Fendoch, was only held until about 87 A.D., but the Romans continued to hold the Lowlands until the end of the century.

Under Agricola a whole network of roads, supply-bases and forts were built. Across the Tyne-Solway gap the Stanegate road was constructed, with an important base at Corbridge at its east end. Dere Street, the main supply road to Scotland, was built north from York, through West Durham to Corbridge, then up the North Tyne and Rede valleys and over the Cheviots to the major Scottish base at Newstead. Northumbrian forts were established at High Rochester (*Bremenium*), north of Otterburn, at Blakehope, slightly to the south, and at Chew Green, high up on the border line. This last fort, a bleak posting for any Roman soldier, was probably to house a few men and horses to help convoys over this difficult stretch of road.

Another road was built from north of Corbridge, travelling north-east towards Berwick through Ryal, Hartburn, and Bridge of Aln. The Devil's Causeway, as the road is known, was partly intended to supply a base at Tweedmouth that was never completed, but was also designed to police the native population. In the late 1930s parts of the road were surveyed and excavated by R. P. Wright, revealing a road about 20 feet wide, with kerbstones, a central rib and a cambered surfacing of sandstone over well-prepared foundations. Some stretches, such as that over Rimside Moor to Edlingham, can still be easily followed across the landscape. Bridges on the road were probably wooden, and in 1834 the local antiquary John Hodgson noted that at Hartburn there was 'a double row of square holes still remaining in the bed of the Hart for fixing it in'. A lateral road running from High Rochester to Bridge of Aln through Holystone and Callaly joined Dere Street to the Causeway. Close to the junction a fort was built at Low Learchild. This may be the *Alauna* of the

Ravenna Cosmography, a gazetteer of the Roman world, and there may be another fort, referred to as *Coccuveda* in the *Cosmography*, still to be found on the Coquetdale Road.

After the Scottish lowlands were evacuated, the forts along the Stanegate were heavily garrisoned. To what extent Northumberland continued to be held is uncertain; the very limited pottery evidence from Learchild fort suggests early 2nd-century occupation, and it may be the present Border rather than the Tyne-Solway line that was the frontier. After 120 A.D., however, the frontier was very definitely drawn across the Tyne-Solway isthmus with the construction of Hadrian's Wall.

The Wall, designed by Hadrian, and built between 122 and 128 is the best-known Roman remain in Britain. Originally designed to start at *Pons Aelius* (Newcastle), it was to run westwards through the Tyne gap, taking advantage of the fine, north-facing scarps of the Whin Sill that give the Wall its most exciting stretches (Plate 4), to Bowness on the Solway. Milecastles were planned for every 1620 yards, with the main garrisons behind the Wall, but easily called up, advancing beyond the Wall through the milecastle gates. During the building of the Wall, however, the design was altered. Construction had almost reached the North Tyne from the east when it was decided to bring the main forts and garrisons up onto the Wall itself. Where possible these forts projected beyond the Wall, the main side gates as well as the north gate leading to the outland, emphasising that the strategy was not to fight from the Wall itself, but to make sorties beyond it. Along the length of the Wall a large ditch, now known as the Vallum, was dug behind it in the middle of a 100-foot cleared strip of ground. This was only crossable at controlled causeways, and enabled a frontier or Wall zone to be defined. The Wall was built by the IInd, VIth and XXth legions, though the operational Wall was manned by auxiliaries from various parts of the Empire. The VIth legion came by sea from Lower Germany in 122, and two stone inscriptions set up to Neptune and Oceanus on their safe arrival have been dredged out of the Tyne near Newcastle Swing Bridge. In the hinterland behind the Wall, forts like Corbridge became redundant, whilst none of the forts beyond the Wall in Northumberland were occupied.

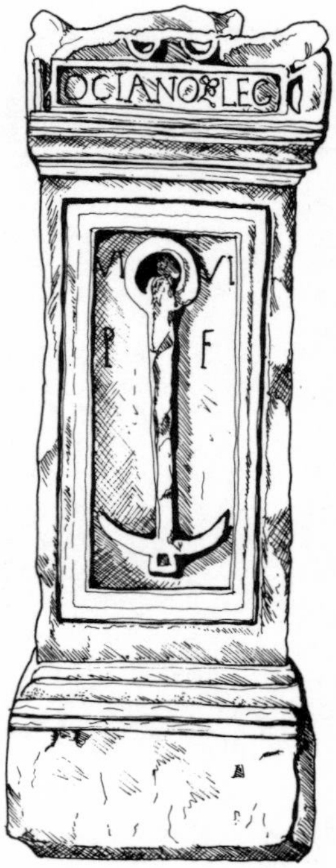

Altar to Oceanus

Although a tactical success, Hadrian's Wall created strategic problems. Potential enemies were free to combine north of the Wall, whilst friendly groups, like the Votadini of Northumberland and East Lothian, were left without protection. The result was a re-advance into Scotland in the reign of Antoninus Pius. Dere Street was re-occupied, new building put up at Corbridge, and then a

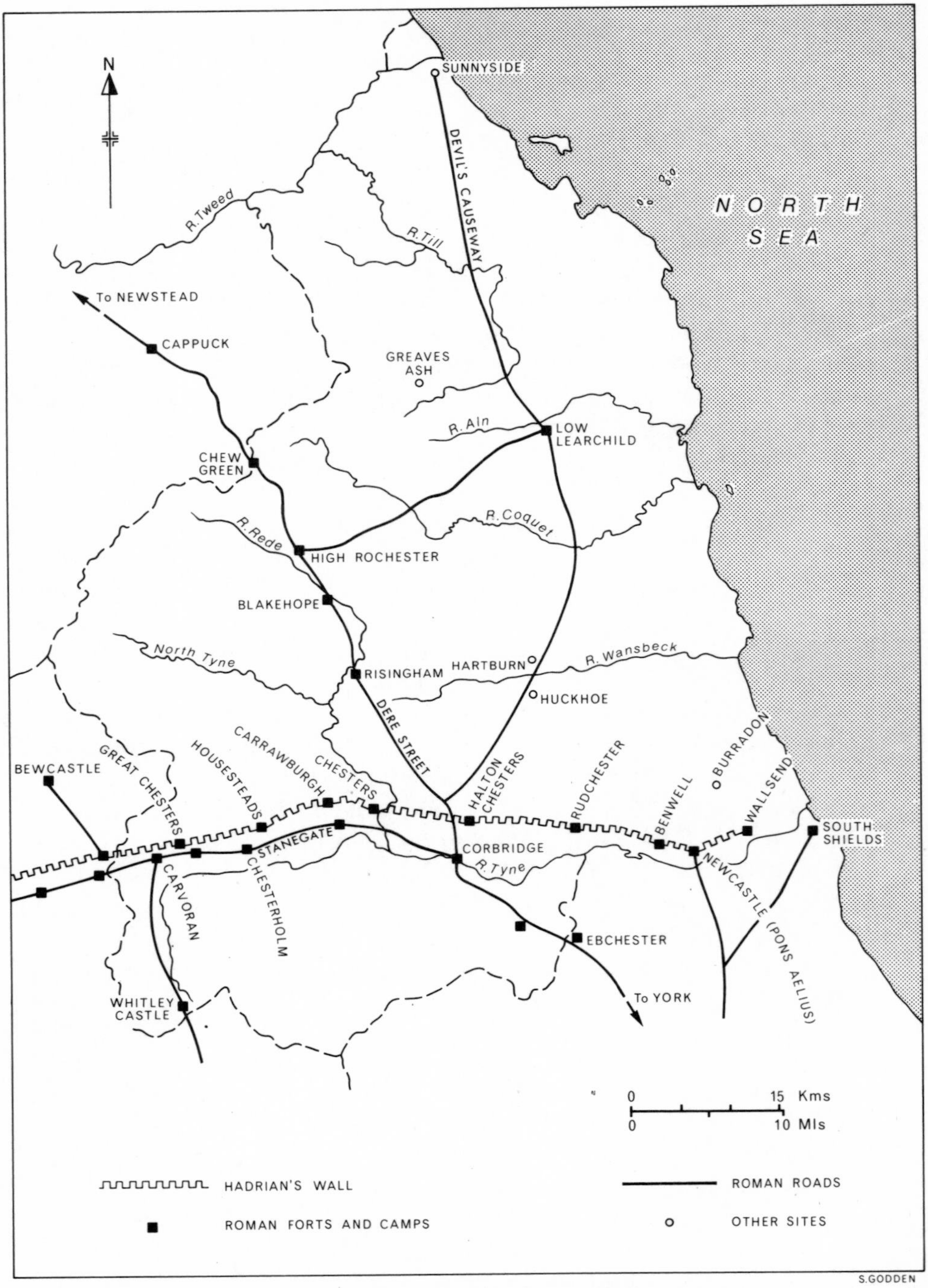
N
NORTH SEA
SUNNYSIDE
DEVIL'S CAUSEWAY
R. Tweed
R. Till
To NEWSTEAD
CAPPUCK
GREAVES ASH
R. Aln
LOW LEARCHILD
CHEW GREEN
R. Coquet
R. Rede
HIGH ROCHESTER
BLAKEHOPE
North Tyne
HARTBURN
R. Wansbeck
RISINGHAM
HUCKHOE
DERE STREET
BURRADON
BEWCASTLE
GREAT CHESTERS
HOUSESTEADS
CARRAWBURGH
CHESTERS
HALTON CHESTERS
RUDCHESTER
BENWELL
WALLSEND
SOUTH SHIELDS
STANEGATE
CORBRIDGE
R. Tyne
CARVORAN
CHESTERHOLM
NEWCASTLE (PONS AELIUS)
EBCHESTER
WHITLEY CASTLE
To YORK
0
15 Kms
0
10 Mls
HADRIAN'S WALL
ROMAN ROADS
ROMAN FORTS AND CAMPS
OTHER SITES
S.GODDEN

2. Roman Northumberland

turf wall, the Antonine Wall, was constructed on the Forth-Clyde line in 142. On the Northumbrian stretch of Dere Street, High Rochester was re-commissioned. An inscribed stone from the fort, now at Alnwick Castle, records this rebuilding by the first mounted cohort of Lingones, a tribe from the East-Gaulish district of Langres. A new fort at Risingham (*Habitancum*) was built between Corbridge and High Rochester to guard the crossing of the river Rede. Chew Green was re-occupied, and the road fitted with milestones. One survivor, marking the twelfth Roman mile north from Corbridge, can now be seen on Waterfalls Hill to the east of the road (Plate 21). On Hadrian's Wall itself, the forts were largely de-garrisoned, the Vallum breached to give easy access, and in the forts and milecastles the gates were torn down. In some milecastles the broken pivot stones can be traced.

The Antonine advance once more brought the Northumberland area within Roman occupation, and it is from this date onwards that Roman influences on native settlement come. The field survey and excavations of G. Jobey have shown that during the Roman period the native settlements of the Votadini became less defensive. The ramparts of the hillforts are often overlain by scattered huts, frequently stone-built, sited particularly on the more sheltered eastern slopes. A good example occurs at Lordenshaws near Rothbury. Other non-defensive settlements sprang up away from the hillforts, around the North Tyne and Rede valleys and in south-east Northumberland. A major village of at least 30 huts exists at Greaves Ash in the Breamish Valley. The aerial photograph (Plate 3) shows Hartburn during excavation by G. Jobey in 1971. The bottom left hut, circular and timber-built, yielded Roman coarse pottery of both late first and second century date. Roman objects did not reach these native sites in any bulk, but continued in a trickle, in some cases, as at Huckhoe, a few miles to the south, right through to the fourth century.

The two main types of Roman pottery found in excavations are coarse pottery, often made in Britain and usually only dateable by typology and association, and Samian pottery, a brilliant red-glazed pottery imported from Gaul. Samian was usually either decorated or, if plain, stamped with the potter's name, so it is usually closely dateable. Mortaria or kitchen mixing-bowls were also by custom stamped by the potter, as with the Halton Chesters bowl stamped *Camulacus fecit*, 'Camulacus made it', an early Hadrianic piece probably made in kilns near Bedford. This detailed ceramic evidence is often crucial in determining the occupation history of sites: lack of Central Gaulish Samian ware was used by Pryce and Birley in the 1930s to confirm the Scottish evacuation around 100 A.D. Similarly

Potter's stamp, Halton Chesters

pottery has been central to recent re-writing of the Antonine period in the north.

The Romans abandoned the Antonine Wall in about 155, possibly because of a revolt south of Hadrian's Wall. In 157–158 many forts on Hadrian's Wall were being re-commissioned, but in 159–160 the Antonine Wall was re-occupied and Hadrian's Wall again largely evacuated, though left in working order. Two years later Calpurnius Agricola was sent to Britain to meet a threatening situation. Until 1972 the general view was that occupation of the Antonine Wall continued until about 180, but B. R. Hartley has used the Samian pottery finds to suggest a re-interpretation. He showed that the stamps of potters working in 140–160 were (as expected) absent from most of Hadrian's Wall, but present on the Antonine Wall, whereas stamps definitely dateable to after 165 (for example those found in a shipwreck of brand-new Samian pottery on the Kent coast at Pudding Pan Rock) were absent from the Antonine Wall. This Wall was abandoned by Calpurnius Agricola in 163 in favour of Hadrian's Wall.

This new picture creates its own problems. Newstead was held as an outpost until about 180. Presumably Dere Street was also held, but the 1930s excavations along it were not geared to this question, and there is a need to re-investigate Risingham, Chew Green and High Rochester to gain more pottery evidence. Also a major destruction at Corbridge and Halton Chesters, previously dated to 197, must now be dated to about 180. Yet the rebuilding by Severus in the first decade of the third century when he campaigned in the north following further enemy invasions, was over 20 years later. Did parts of the frontier lie derelict for this time?

After 211 there was a long period of relative peace. The Severan reconstruction revised the frontier strategy, and a strong emphasis was placed on outposts beyond the Wall. Artillery defences were built at High Rochester and Risingham. In addition, long-range scouts or *exploratores* toured the Cheviots area, reporting on hostile movements, and keeping contact with friendly groups. At Sunnyside, south of Tweedmouth, pottery from a late third-century mortarium has been found, probably left by scouts patrolling up the Devil's Causeway. In this period local recruiting to the auxiliaries became common, linking the soldiers to the local population; they were also allowed to marry and lease lands. This was the main age of civilian settlements or *vici* in the frontier zone. The highly developed urban life of southern Roman Britain had no place in the frontier zone, nor did the villa (though there was a villa at Old Durham), but around the military camps civilian settlements grew up, as at Corbridge, Chesterholm and

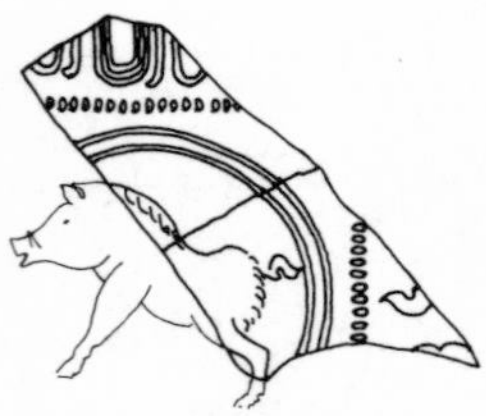

Samian pottery fragment, Corbridge

Housesteads. At Chesterholm (*Vindolanda*), north of Bardon Mill, there have been major excavations in the last nine years by Robin Birley. This *vicus* was self-governing, with shops, workshops, and a large 15-room courtyard house, probably designed for travelling Roman officials.

In 296 Roman troops were withdrawn to fight for the usurping Allectus, and the northern tribes took advantage to destroy as far south as York and Chester. There is, however, little dateable evidence after 276 and much of the destruction may date from then. The new Emperor Constantius, who defeated Allectus in the south, reacted swiftly, and the frontier was soon recontrolled and new building took place. But north of the Wall, at Risingham, for example, the *vici* were no longer inhabited. In 343 the outposts at Risingham and High Rochester were burnt down in an invasion not of British tribes, but of Picts from north of the Tay. In the excavations at Risingham the red calcined threshold to the west gate provided clear evidence of this burning. After this High Rochester was abandoned, but Risingham kept because the local iron-ore deposits were needed for the military forges at Corbridge. Twenty-five years later, in 367, a 'barbarian conspiracy' of hostile groups, aided by treachery of the scouts, again destroyed the frontier.

Bronze military standard, Vindolanda

After this incursion the frontier was restored by Theodosius, but it was no longer based on Roman military might. The remaining outposts were abandoned, and the Wall and forts rather chaotically restored by what were now soldier-settlers, not military garrisons. The *vici* contracted, though Corbridge and *Vindolanda* remained into the fifth century. A key element in the new policy was the relationship with treaty-states of the Votadini and other tribes beyond the Wall. There was no dramatic leaving-ceremony on the Roman Wall: by the time of formal Roman withdrawal from Britain in 410, the local inhabitants were dominant on the frontier. There was no collapse of order, and the Britons showed a capacity for organised policy, evidenced by the migration of a group from Manau, a treaty-state around what is now Clackmannan, to North Wales to drive out Irish invaders. But the Roman elements, particularly the urban life of the *vici*, did not last long in this thinly-Romanised frontier zone.

IV Anglo-Saxon Northumberland

Anglian cross fragment, Alnmouth

After the Roman departure from the northern frontier, the region was controlled by a number of small British Kingdoms. Little archaeological evidence of this period has been found, though the Romano-British settlement at Huckhoe near Bolam revealed pottery of late 5th- or early 6th-century date that probably came by trade from west of the Pennines, possibly with the Dalriadic Scots of Argyll and Ulster. The Votadini groups held Northumberland until the mid-sixth century, when Anglians, already well established further south in Yorkshire, began arriving on the coast. In about 547 Ida and his followers came by sea from Yorkshire and established a beachhead at Bamburgh. For a considerable time the British forces contained these invaders in a few coastal sites. 'Outigern fought bravely against the race of the English', one record reads. Urbgen of Rheged, a British territory focussed on Carlisle, besieged the Angle Theodric for three days and nights on Lindisfarne sometime between 571 and 578. It was only with the accession of Aethelfrith towards the close of the century that this new kingdom of Bernicia took real hold of Northumberland and expanded outwards.

This chronology is confirmed by the place-name and archaeological evidence. There are few pagan (i.e., early Anglian) cemeteries in Northumberland, the most notable at Howick on the coast, and only one example of the -ingas place-name (Birling near Warkworth) that characterises early settlement in southern England. In the following century the Anglians spread across the country, establishing villages and fields, clearing wood and marsh. Second phase names ending in -ingham, meaning homestead of the people of, are common and occupy good sites in river valleys. From settlements such as Ellingham, Chillingham and Ovingham, further settlements sprang up, as at Ovington next to Ovingham. It is difficult, if not impossible, to know to what extent they took over a Celtic or British landscape or created a new one. Certainly the names frequently suggest the clearing of new ground: Hedgeley, meaning Hiddi's clearing; Fenham, homestead in the marsh; Shipley, sheep clearing.

Many British elements persisted, however, as at Wallington, farm of the sons of the Briton or Welshman, and especially amongst the higher ground that did not become a landscape of large villages. The river names are all Celtic, as are Mindrum, Plenmeller ('top of the bare hill'), Ross, Troughend and Glendue ('black or dark valley'). Cambois, near Blyth, is a Normanised form of Celtic Camus, bay. Many Celtic personal-names survived in use until the 12th and 13th centuries. A Wesescop (meaning 'Bishop's lad') is found in Tynedale, a Gillemichel at Longframlington, and a Gillefani at Hethpool. Prof. G. W. S. Barrow, who noted these survivals, has also drawn attention to the parallels in land organisation and tenure between Anglian Northumbria and Celtic areas in Scotland and Wales, suggesting the Angles did not re-start from scratch. Dr. Alcock, the archaeologist, goes further: '. . . in Bernicia a very small, and largely aristocratic, Anglian element ruled over a predominantly British population', though this perhaps overstates the case.

There is no need here to chronicle the tremendous expansion of the Bernician kingdom in the century after Aethelfrith's victory over the Scots at Degsastan in 603. In that century Northumbria came to extend from the Humber and Mersey in the south to the Solway in the north west and the Firth of Forth in the north east. Lothian became an Anglian area. In this period Northumbria was a major political and cultural centre with links throughout Europe. For most of this period Northumbria was ruled by the Bernician royal house, but after Aethelfrith's death the throne was secured by Edwin of Deira (the Anglian kingdom of York) and the Bernician family sought exile in Scotland, though they returned under Oswald after Edwin's death.

The Angles were not Christians, unlike the British. However, Edwin's wife was from the Kentish royal family that had been converted by Augustine and Paulinus. Paulinus was invited north, and he converted and baptized throughout Northumbria. He came to the royal estate of Yeavering near Wooler, and for 36 days preached and baptized in the River Glen. Aerial photography by J. K. St. Joseph in 1949 identified a possible site for this royal palace at Yeavering, called *Ad Gefrin* by Bede, and it has since been excavated by Brian Hope-Taylor. A whole series of halls have been revealed, in form like the great hall of *Heorot* described in the poem *Boewulf,* together with an amphitheatre which may have been used for councils and where Paulinus may have preached. Later another hall at *Maelmin,* two miles away at Milfield, succeeded it.

The return of the exiled Oswald brought Celtic monks from Iona to Lindisfarne under Aidan. There were organisational conflicts between the Celtic and Roman groups, eventually decided in favour of the Roman group, but the Celtic missions had great influence. The years 650 to 750 were the golden age of Northumbrian monasticism under bishops like Cuthbert of Lindisfarne and Wilfred of Hexham.

Bishop's seat, Hexham

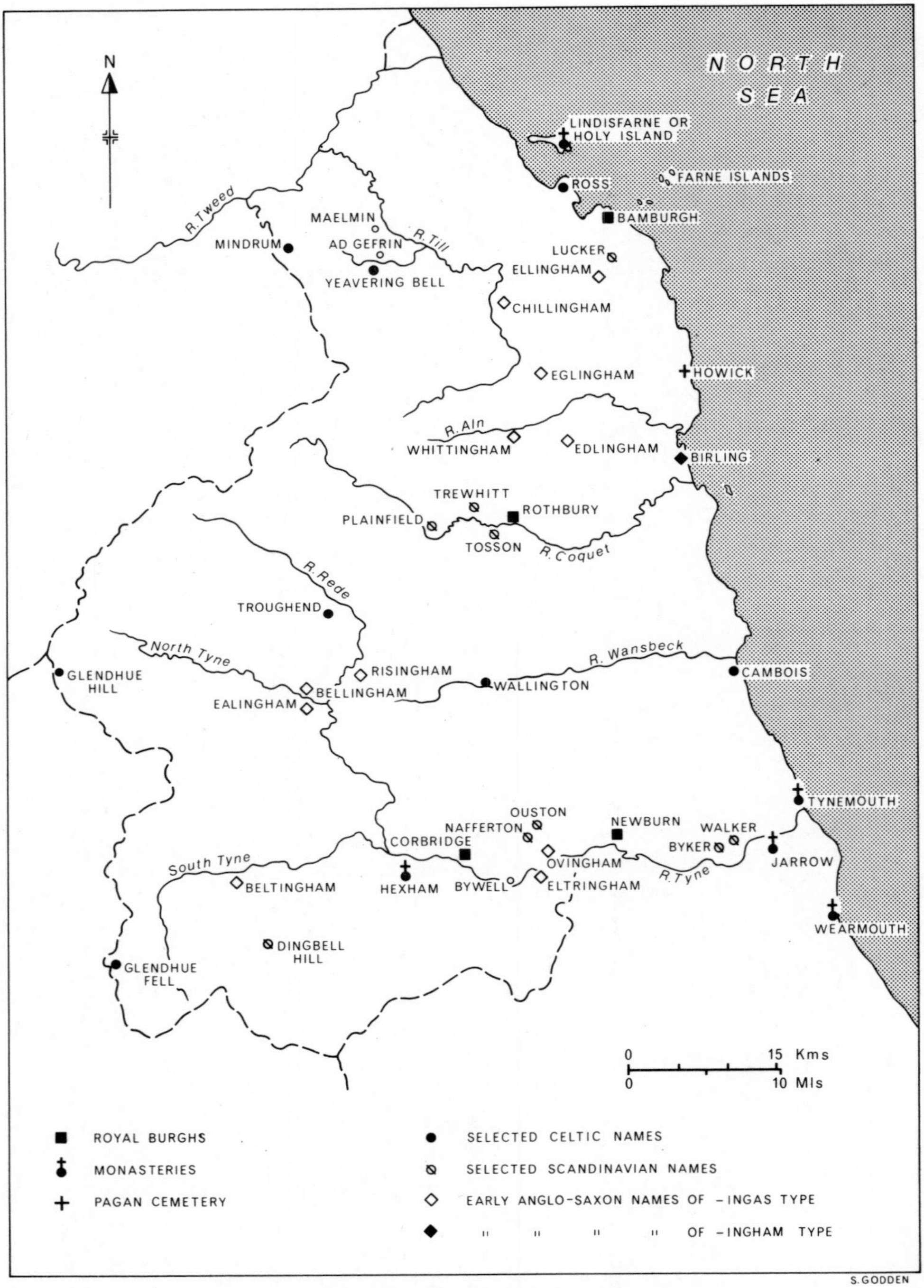
N
NORTH SEA
LINDISFARNE OR HOLY ISLAND
FARNE ISLANDS
ROSS
BAMBURGH
R. Tweed
MAELMIN
AD GEFRIN
R. Till
MINDRUM
YEAVERING BELL
LUCKER
ELLINGHAM
CHILLINGHAM
EGLINGHAM
HOWICK
R. Aln
WHITTINGHAM
EDLINGHAM
BIRLING
TREWHITT
ROTHBURY
PLAINFIELD
TOSSON
R. Coquet
R. Rede
TROUGHEND
North Tyne
R. Wansbeck
GLENDHUE HILL
RISINGHAM
BELLINGHAM
WALLINGTON
CAMBOIS
EALINGHAM
TYNEMOUTH
OUSTON
NAFFERTON
NEWBURN
WALKER
CORBRIDGE
BYKER
JARROW
South Tyne
OVINGHAM
R. Tyne
BELTINGHAM
HEXHAM
BYWELL
ELTRINGHAM
WEARMOUTH
DINGBELL HILL
GLENDHUE FELL
0 15 Kms
0 10 Mls
ROYAL BURGHS
MONASTERIES
PAGAN CEMETERY
SELECTED CELTIC NAMES
SELECTED SCANDINAVIAN NAMES
EARLY ANGLO-SAXON NAMES OF -INGAS TYPE
" " " " OF -INGHAM TYPE
S.GODDEN

3. Anglo-Saxon Northumberland

Cuthbert, the shepherd-boy from the Lammermuirs, belonged to the ascetic, itinerant Celtic school, spending over nine years as a hermit on the Inner Farne, eventually returning there to die (Plate 6). Wilfred, for a time Bishop of all Northumbria, was a more political figure, acquiring lands and influence for the Church, but his ambition created enemies and led to his demotion. He founded the monastery at Hexham in the 660s and the lands of Hexhamshire were granted to it by Queen Aethelthryth in about 674. From this period date the *Lindisfarne Gospels*, with their blend of Celtic, Germanic and Romanesque art, and the works of Bede and others in monasteries at Jarrow, Monkwearmouth, Lindisfarne, Tynemouth and elsewhere. Lindisfarne has recently been suggested as a possible origin for the *Book of Kells*, and D. R. Howlett has argued very convincingly that the Anglo-Latin poem *De Abbatibus* was written by the monk Aethelwulf at Bywell-on-Tyne about 819.

Anglian cross fragment, Rothbury

In the 8th century Northumbrian political power declined. There was much internal dissension. Bede notes in the 730s that spurious monasteries were created, where laymen and their families, including most government officials, profited by their exemption from secular services. Their personal gain resulted in a weak state, unable to defend itself, as Bede had predicted.

The Danish pirates first arrived on the coast in 793. *The Anglo-Saxon Chronicle* records: 'In this year dire portents appeared over Northumbria and sorely frightened the people. They consisted of immense whirlwinds and flashes of lightning, and fiery dragons were seen flying in the air. A great famine immediately followed those signs, and a little after that in the same year, on 8th June, the ravages of heathen men miserably destroyed God's church on Lindisfarne, with plunder and slaughter'. Jarrow was attacked the following year. However, the main Danish invasions did not come until 70 years later, and came in south-east England. After a year they occupied York (866) and in 874 one of the Danish leaders, Halfdan, led an expedition to the north, and sailed into the Tyne. They ravaged Northumberland, destroyed Tynemouth monastery, and set up winter quarters. In the new year 'Halfdan shared out the lands of the Northumbrians, and they proceeded to plough and support themselves'.

This Danish settlement took place almost entirely south of the Tees. There are only a few Scandinavian place-names in Northumberland, such as Byker ('village by the marsh'), Walker, a few names in the south west, like Ouston, the farm of Ulfr, and Nafferton, the farm of the man nicknamed 'Night-traveller', and a possible group around Rothbury. Sir Edmund Craster noted some interesting evidence of Danish settlement at Tynemouth, where personal

Bolam church

names like Orm, Svan, Hedne, and Hrother are found in the 11th century. For the most part the Danes left the rump of Northumbria north of the Tees as a virtually independent kingdom, which became a rather isolated Anglian region.

However, the Danish invasions destroyed Northumbrian monasticism and church organisation. The bishop and monks of Lindisfarne fled before Halfdan's Danes, and, together with the relics of St. Cuthbert, roamed the countryside for seven years until they settled at Chester-le-Street, moving to Durham a hundred years later. The see of Hexham was also extinguished and monasticism did not return until after the Norman Conquest, though a church revival in the 11th century has left a number of fine Anglo-Saxon churches, as at Ovingham (Plate 7) and Bywell.

The Northumbrian kingdom, centred on Bamburgh, was a weak element in the fight that the West Saxons led against the Danes. It lost territory to other expansionist groups: Norsemen took Lancashire and Cumbria; Strathclyde took around the Solway; by 850 the newly-formed kingdom of Scotland was capturing Anglian Lothian, and by 945 was established up to the Tweed. The success of the West Saxons led to the subordination of the Northumbrian kingdom to them in 927, and in 954 it became the Northumbrian earldom. By this time the Scots had carried the war south of the Tweed, and in 969 Malcolm 'devastated the province of the Northumbrians with the sword and fire': the question was now whether the Anglo-Scottish border could be pushed south to the Tyne.

5. *Vindolanda* (Chesterholm) Roman fort under light snow. The site of the recently excavated *vicus* lies just beyond the fort.

6. St. Cuthbert on the Inner Farne, from the Durham manuscript (*c.*1200) of Bede's *Life of St. Cuthbert*.

7. Ovingham church. A late Anglo-Saxon church tower in an early Anglo-Saxon village.

8. Elsdon castle. A motte-and-bailey castle built by the Umfravilles of Redesdale.

V The Norman Conquest and Feudal Northumberland

After the Norman Conquest of 1066, William I and his son William Rufus tried to continue the rule of Northumberland through the earldom. It was not a successful policy. A whole succession of native and Norman earls were either murdered or led rebellions themselves, despite a punitive devastation of northern lands by William in 1080. When Eilaf the hereditary priest of Hexham went there shortly after, there was no cultivation and for two years he had to support his family by hunting. After Robert Mowbray's rebellion in the 1090s, in which he was besieged in Bamburgh Castle, the earldom was suppressed and its lands taken by the King, who began to grant them to his followers.

Under Henry I these grants were extensive. The Granvills got the barony of Ellingham, the de Umfravilles Prudhoe, the Muschamps Wooler, the de Vescis Alnwick. These Norman barons in turn granted parts of their estates to others, many from Norman families already settled in Yorkshire. The de Vescis, and the Tisons, to whom they granted Shilbottle, are examples. In 1166 Craster was held for a knight's fee by Albert de Crawcestre, who probably came from the Cleveland district of Yorkshire. Many of the earliest surviving castles date from this period. The Bertrams built the motte-and-bailey castle at Mitford, initially of wood and soil, but by 1138 it had the curtain-wall that can still be seen. The Umfravilles built Elsdon, and the Bishop of Durham a castle at Norham to protect his estates by the Tweed.

A major problem was the expansionist Scots. In the 11th century they had invaded at any time of Norman political weakness, and after Henry I's death in 1135 they intervened in the civil war that followed. David of Scotland invaded through Northumberland, but was defeated at Northallerton in 1138. By the treaty of 1139 the earldom of Northumberland was given to the heir to the Scots' throne, who claimed it as heir to earl Waltheof, the last native earl. In 1157 Henry II took back the earldom, later giving the dispossessed earl Tynedale as compensation, to be held as an independent regality by homage only. When William the Lion became Scots' king in 1165 Henry refused him the earldom. William invaded in 1174, but was unable to capture Alnwick and Wark. He was captured at Alnwick, at the same time as Duncan of Fife was burning the town of Warkworth

Seal of Henry II

Arms of Roger of Warkworth

and killing the inhabitants, including those who took refuge in St. Lawrence's church. The defeat of William the Lion gave Northumberland a century of relative peace on the border until 1296.

The Norman take-over was one of aristocratic transplantation, not large-scale immigration. In 1166 there were 21 barons and 64 knights in the county, and not all of these were Normans. W. P. Hedley, the Northumbrian genealogist, has estimated that, with all their retainers, the Normans in Northumberland totalled less than four hundred. Because Norman settlement took place some 50 years later here than further south, many more Anglo-Saxon landowners survived in Northumberland.

Under the Norman feudal system, the King granted land to barons in return for military service. The barons, in their turn, might grant part of their estates to knights, also in return for military service. In the old Anglo-Saxon system there was no such formal relation between land-holding and duties to the King or earl. Below the earl there were the thanes, who held groups of villages or 'shires', and the drengs, who held smaller villages or townships, and had to do more menial services for them. As Prof. Barrow notes, 'it is probable that most of the baronies of Northumberland were created out of land previously held in thanage'. Baronies might vary greatly in size and contain different numbers of knights' fees. In 1166 the de Vesci barony of Alnwick contained 13 knights' fees, whereas Roger of Warkworth had sub-granted none of his barony.

A number of thanages and drengships survived, however. In 1166 there were two thanages, at Halton near Corbridge, and at Hepple in upper Coquetdale. Drengships still existed at Whittingham and Eslington, and at Mousen and Beadnell near Bamburgh, and at Throckley near Newburn. These had probably survived through relation to royal lands: the royal boroughs of Bamburgh and Newburn and a complicated assemblage of crown lands in Whittingham Vale. The services of a drengship were fairly menial: the dreng of Mousen had to pay a rent of 30s., carry 15 tree trunks a year to Bamburgh, and plough, carry and reap on the demesne lands at Bamburgh. Over the years, however, these Saxon survivals were put under pressure to conform to the Norman system. Thanes and drengs had to pay heavy taxes, notably the cornage, that knights were exempt from, and from 1159 to 1169 a sizeable cornage was demanded every other year. Gradually, the tenures were altered to knights' fees, or, in one case, a barony.

There were also social influences. Norman names became fashionable. Before 1161, Waltheof of Hepple had been succeeded by his son William. But the Anglo-Saxon Liulfs, Waltheofs, Maldreds and

Uchtreds survived a long time, especially in the lower ranks of society, and the 1296 Lay Subsidy Roll for the county lists many of them. In later years only a few Northumbrian families could trace their ancestry back to native families (notably the Gospatrics; others are the Ildertons and Roddams, but these do not date back to 1066), but this is because the early records are poor and only encompass the highest ranks of society. The vast bulk of the population was of pre-Norman origin, a mixture of Anglian, Celtic, and, to a much lesser extent, Scandinavian stock.

Arms of Ilderton

The actual working of the land continued to be done by this native population, whether bonds or neyfs. The latter were definitely unfree, but the status of bonds is often difficult to determine. The basic feudal services in the Norman system were an obligation to work the lord's lands, or demesne, in return for the right to work land for yourself. In 1295 John Miller of Preston in Tynemouth held 36 acres as a bond of the prior of Tynemouth. His duties included two days' work each week on the demesne, ploughing, harrowing and seeding. At harvest he had to reap two days a week, bringing two other labourers with him, cart the harvest to the manorial grange, and help thresh wheat daily in the prior's barn. He also had to take his own corn to the manorial mill. But the classic village manorial system sat uneasily on the shire-based heritage of Northumberland, and many of the feudal duties were relics of pre-Conquest services to a mobile roual court: carting goods, food-rents and hospitality, and seasonal agricultural work, but little weekly labour on a demesne. At Shoreston in Bamburghshire the duties included carrying goods on horseback between the Coquet and the Tweed, and on the journey they were allowed bread and one drink. In 1245 they complained that in the last seven years they had had no food on these journeys, which numbered 1,440, or over 200 a year.

The landowners were keen to retain or increase their numbers of unfree serfs, and there are many legal cases over whether a man was free or unfree. At the 1256 Assizes, Henry, the dreng of Mousen, claimed two brothers, Adam and Walter, were his fugitive serfs or neyfs. Fortunately, they were able to show that their grandfather, Walter Coltebayn, was an immigrant from Flanders, and that they were free men. William of Killingworth was less lucky, and was delivered with all his family and goods to his master, Galfridus of Weteslade, at the same Assize. In 1292 Richard of Craster claimed a man named William as a fugitive serf, even producing William's brother, who admitted he was unfree. William denied this, saying his grandfather was a free man who had migrated to Craster from

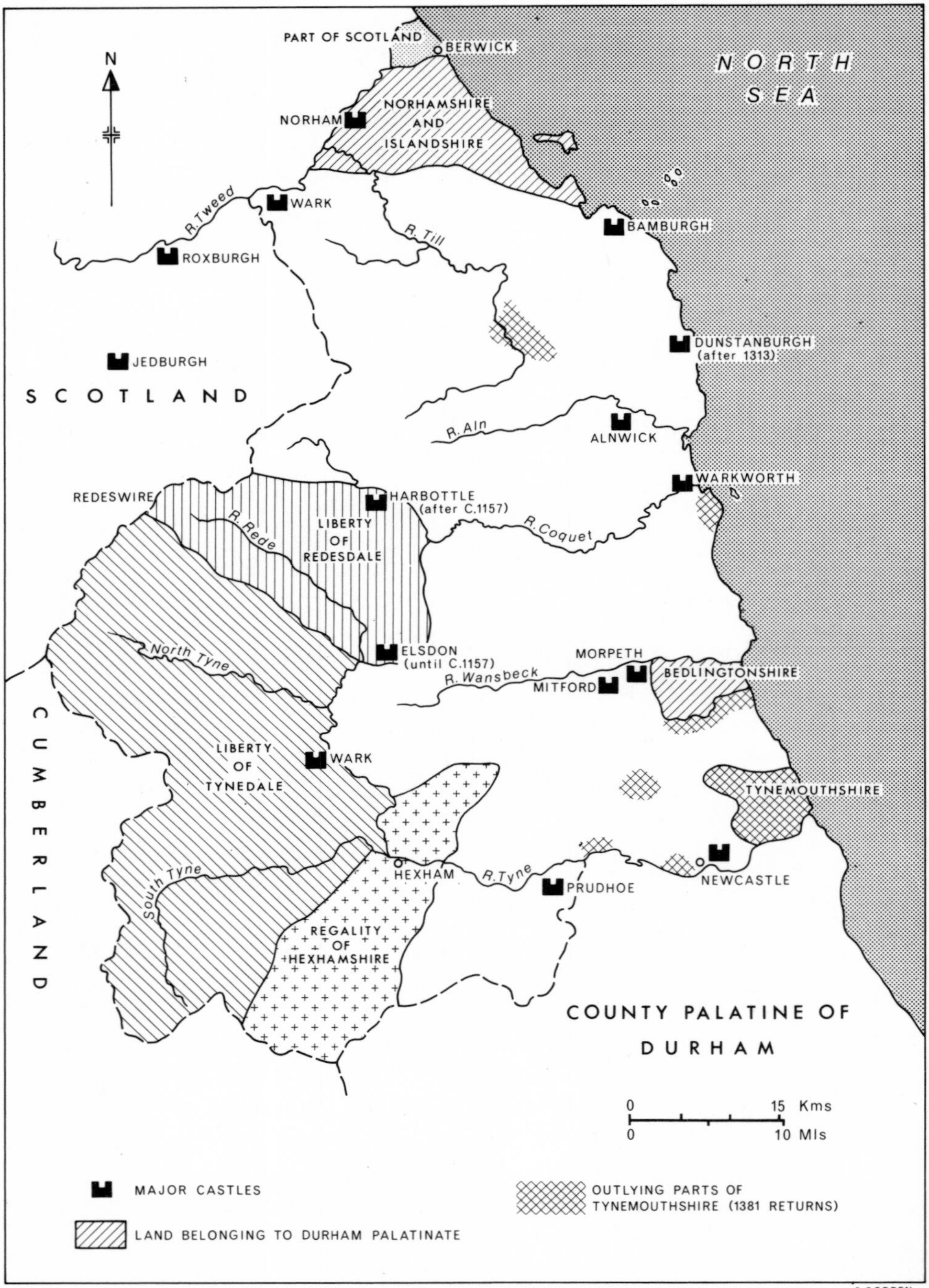

PART OF SCOTLAND
BERWICK
NORTH SEA
N
NORHAM
NORHAMSHIRE AND ISLANDSHIRE
R. Tweed
WARK
ROXBURGH
R. Till
BAMBURGH
DUNSTANBURGH (after 1313)
JEDBURGH
SCOTLAND
R. Aln
ALNWICK
WARKWORTH
REDESWIRE
HARBOTTLE (after C.1157)
LIBERTY OF REDESDALE
R. Rede
R. Coquet
North Tyne
ELSDON (until C.1157)
MORPETH
R. Wansbeck
MITFORD
BEDLINGTONSHIRE
CUMBERLAND
LIBERTY OF TYNEDALE
WARK
TYNEMOUTHSHIRE
South Tyne
HEXHAM
R. Tyne
PRUDHOE
NEWCASTLE
REGALITY OF HEXHAMSHIRE
COUNTY PALATINE OF DURHAM
0 15 Kms
0 10 Mls
MAJOR CASTLES
OUTLYING PARTS OF TYNEMOUTHSHIRE (1381 RETURNS)
LAND BELONGING TO DURHAM PALATINATE
S.GODDEN

4. Medieval Northumberland

Acklington and that his brother might also be free had he not made 'his foolish confession'. William won, and Richard acknowledged his family's freedom.

The whole of Northumberland was not split into military baronies. Some estates were held for official services, like the south Northumberland coroner's lands at Nafferton and West Maften. Extensive lands were held by the church in Tynemouthshire, Hexhamshire (belonging to the archbishopric of York), and the Durham bishopric, which had estates along the Tweed and near Lindisfarne as Norhamshire and Islandshire, as well as Bedlingtonshire in south-east Northumberland. Each of these were 'liberties' of 'franchises', separate from the administration of the rest of the county. The sheriff and his officers had no powers there. Tynedale was also a liberty in the hands of the Scots' king, and Redesdale was granted to the powerful Umfraville family as a franchise.

Arms of Craster

These separate jurisdictions created problems in the administration of law and justice. This is illustrated by the case of accidental death of Adam Aydrunken (the records also have such names as Robert Pusekat, Robert Unkouth, and Richard Whirlepipyn the minstrel). In the Assize at Wark-on-Tyne in 1279 the Scots' king's justices recorded misadventure when Adam fell out of a boat and drowned. Normally the goods involved in a crime or unnatural death were forfeited to the King's officers as a *deodand,* but in this case the jury said that the boat could not be claimed as it had drifted across to the Northumbrian bank in the King of England's land. More seriously these liberties provided a refuge for criminals because 'the King's writ did not run there'. Crime was probably no greater in Northumberland than elsewhere in England, but it was less often punished. Sanctuary could also be claimed at churches, and the Scottish border was not far away. After sanctuary, the criminal was given the choice of submitting to trial or leaving the country. Tynemouth was notorious for the way the Prior was willing to take wanted men, so when William Faber of Warkworth stabbed Roger Paraventur' in the heart with a knife, he fled to Tynemouth and was outlawed at the 1279 Northumberland Assize. In a seaport brawl Robert of Alnmouth hit William of Lothian on the head with a hatchet whilst on a ship on the river Aln. William died, and Robert fled and was outlawed. The 1256 Assize Roll records the case of Roger, son of Thomas of Easingwold. Roger stole some clothes in Acklington, and, having to flee, he sought sanctuary in the church at Bolam (at that time one of the larger villages in the county). When he was seen by the coroner he opted to leave the country. The village of Acklington was reprimanded for not having given pursuit, and the

Norham Castle

village of Bolam also, for not pursuing him when the hue and cry was raised. Sometimes the criminals were not even identified: two young women, Evota and Femota, were returning from a visit to Mitford through Stobswood forest when they were attacked and robbed by 'unknown malfactors', and although the hue and cry was raised, the robbers got away, and the neighbouring villages were later reprimanded for not giving pursuit. The criminal who was caught could face very summary justice, even the 13th-century form of Lynch Law: William Yrrumpurs burgled a house in Wooler and stole seven skins, but the local men chased and caught him, and promptly beheaded him. When a Gilbert of Niddesdale was crossing a moor with a hermit called Semmanus of Bottelesham, he attacked the hermit, robbing him and leaving him naked and injured. However, Gilbert was arrested on suspicion by Ralph of Belford, a King's serjeant, and taken to Alnwick. The hermit also came to Alnwick, and when Gilbert confessed, the serjeant had the hermit decapitate Gilbert, and the sheriff and coroner both later testified that this was the custom in the county.

As well as the criminal cases, the Assize Rolls contain the coroner's records of tragic deaths. What drove Beatrix de Roddam to hang herself in the tower at Newton-on-the-Moor? The 1256 Assize Roll records that Roger of Swarland took his corn to Felton mill, but was crushed to death by two of the grinding stones. The same Roll also gives the case of Peter Graper of Colewell, who shot an arrow at a pigeon and unfortunately hit Uctred, the carpenter from Bockenfield. Uctred died, and Peter fled and was outlawed, but he later returned and was pardoned as it was an accident. The 1279 Assize records that Thomas of Hoburn was gutting fish at Seaton Delaval when with his knife he accidentally struck on the head a woman begging alms, and killed her.

VI The Medieval Countryside

William the Conqueror's devastation of the north, and his incomplete hold on the region, meant Northumberland, along with other parts of the north, was not included in the great Domesday Survey of 1086. In more southerly parts of England this Survey provides a picture of the countryside at the end of the Anglo-Saxon era and before the great agricultural and commercial expansion of the 12th and 13th centuries. In Northumberland few surviving records are earlier than the 12th century (the oldest royal charter, now in Alnwick Castle, is a grant of Ellingham near Bamburgh by Henry I to Ralph de Gaugy, dated 1120–1133), and it is more difficult to disentangle the Anglo-Saxon and Norman elements in the landscape. However, the place-name evidence indicates that the main features of settlement had been laid down before the Conquest.

Nevertheless, there remained scope for considerable agricultural expansion. In the lowlands the village fields were surrounded by wastes and commons, many right down to the 18th century. There were large tracts of moor, and many areas were still wooded, as around Rothbury and Brinkburn, or in the foothills south of the Tyne. Several parts of the Cheviots were well wooded, and Robert de Umfraville had 300 acres of wood at Kingshope and 100 at Cottonshope in Upper Redesdale. There was room for the early Norman kings to set aside large areas of the county as hunting forests, as occurred around Alnwick, Rothbury, and Felton. These were not dense woodland, for the term 'forest' in this context comes not from the Latin *foresta,* but from *foris*, 'outside', meaning land outside the common law, but they were often overgrown, scrubby or lightly wooded.

In the lowlands there was open-field arable farming. Cultivation was generally in furlongs, often loosely grouped into blocks, and individuals might hold strips in many parts of the unfenced fields. On these plots the main crops were oats and wheat. In Northumberland the climate and soil often did not allow the roughly equal acreages of winter-sown grain, spring grain, and fallow that formed the basis of the regular three-course rotations further south. Such systems probably existed at Bamburgh and Embleton, and in 1232 there was a three-course rotation of rye and wheat, oats and fallow at Hextold. But the acreages for the Knights Templars' estate at

Medieval sowing

Medieval dovecot, Bamburgh

Temple Thornton, near Mitford, in 1308 are probably more typical: there they sowed 37 acres of wheat and 101 acres of oats. They spent £9 8s. 6d. (£9.42½p) on the seed and 5s. 9d. (29p) to have the 138 acres weeded at ½d. (0.2p) an acre. The accounts also detail 12s. (60p) for the repair of ploughs and harrows, and 10d. (4p) for salt for the servants' porridge.

The crops might be mixed up in the village fields, but the problems this created gradually forced farming towards a regular two- or three-field system for a village, each field devoted to one crop or fallow. The sort of problems are illustrated by Henry Fawkes of West Backworth, who sued the Prior of Tynemouth in 1316 for damage caused by the Prior's animals to his corn, but the claim was disallowed because Henry had been cultivating a furlong that should have lain fallow that year.

Pastoral farming was at least as important as arable. In the Temple Thornton accounts are listed 400 sheep, though 97 had died of disease or 'murrain' and 3s. (15p) had been spent on sheep ointment. Two hundred and fifty-three fleeces had been sold. In many areas there were large-scale flocks and herds. During the early fourteenth century there were 3,600 sheep pastured along the lower banks of the Tweed. The Umfravilles had numerous sheep and cattle on the moors of Otterburn and Redesdale, and in 1245 the pasture of Alwinton and Otterburn was estimated to carry 1,140 sheep and 1,400 cows. In the lowlands the animals were grazed on the commons and the fallow, but on the moorlands the sheep and cattle were taken in the summer months to the higher fells of Redesdale, Tynedale and Kidland, the shepherds living in temporary huts or shielings, returning to the valleys in winter. As the human and animal population increased, so the regulation of pasture rights became more important. At the assizes in 1293 the Abbot of Alnwick was sued for exceeding his pasture stint on Edlingham moors. Each tenant of a bovate was allowed two horses, two oxen, two cows, two pigs, and 40 sheep, but the Abbot, who had four bovates, had overstocked to the tune of 1,000 sheep, 200 pigs, 40 oxen, 40 horses, and 40 cows.

Only rarely does the surviving evidence go beyond the manorial duties to the details of peasant living conditions in the medieval farming community. One enquiry after the death of a tenant at Wallsend in 1349 (he had died in the Black Death of that year) reported that he had farmed 23 acres, sowing 10 with wheat, two with barley, and eight with oats and peas. The man's possessions were listed as a plough, two carts, three harrows, an earthenware pot, and a vat, four boars and a cow.

9. Guyzance nunnery at Brainshaugh on the Coquet, established by the Tisons before 1147. After 1313 it became a curacy, and although it passed into private hands after the 1536 Dissolution, it was occasionally used for marriages until the 19th century.

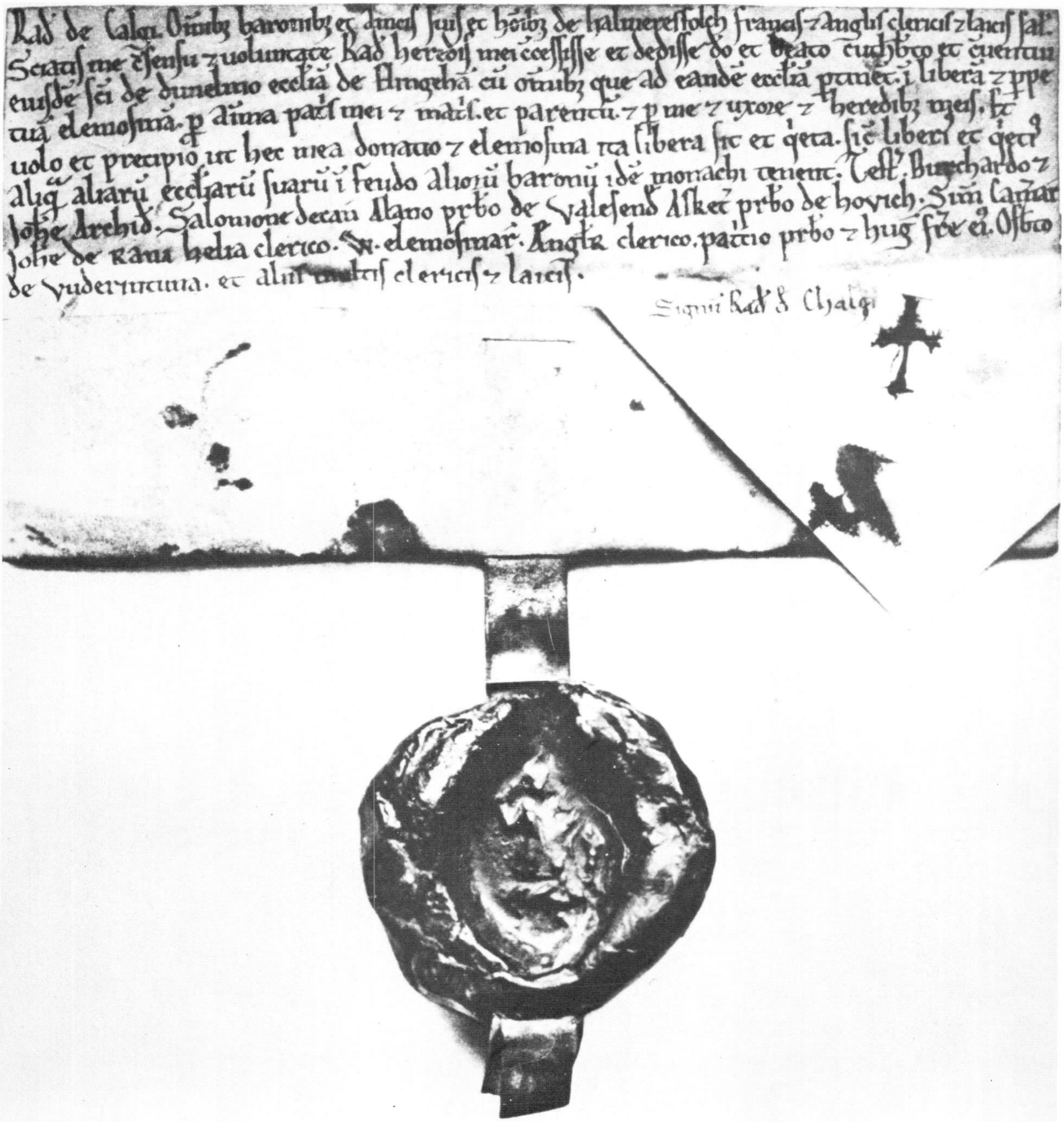

10. Grant (*c.* 1150-57) of Ellingham Church to Durham Priory.

Translation: Ralph de Gaugy greets all barons, his friends, and the men of the holy man's folk [haliueresfolch, i.e. St. Cuthbert's people or the diocese of Durham], French and English, clergy and laity. Let it be known that with the agreement and wish of Ralph, my heir, I have granted and given the church of Ellingham and all that belongs to the church to God and St. Cuthbert and his convent of Durham, as a free and everlasting gift on behalf of the souls of my father, mother and ancestors, and of myself, my wife and my heirs. And I will and order that this my gift and alms be just as freely and quietly held as the monks hold any other churches in the fee of other barons.

The grant is witnessed by a number of clerics, and Ralph de Gaugy has put his mark in the shape of a cross, which has been made with labour and difficulty.

11. St. Lawrence's Church, Warkworth. A Norman church, in which the rebels prayed for 'King James III' in 1715.

12. Dunstanburgh Castle, the Gatehouse. The castle was begun by Thomas, Earl of Lancaster, in 1313.

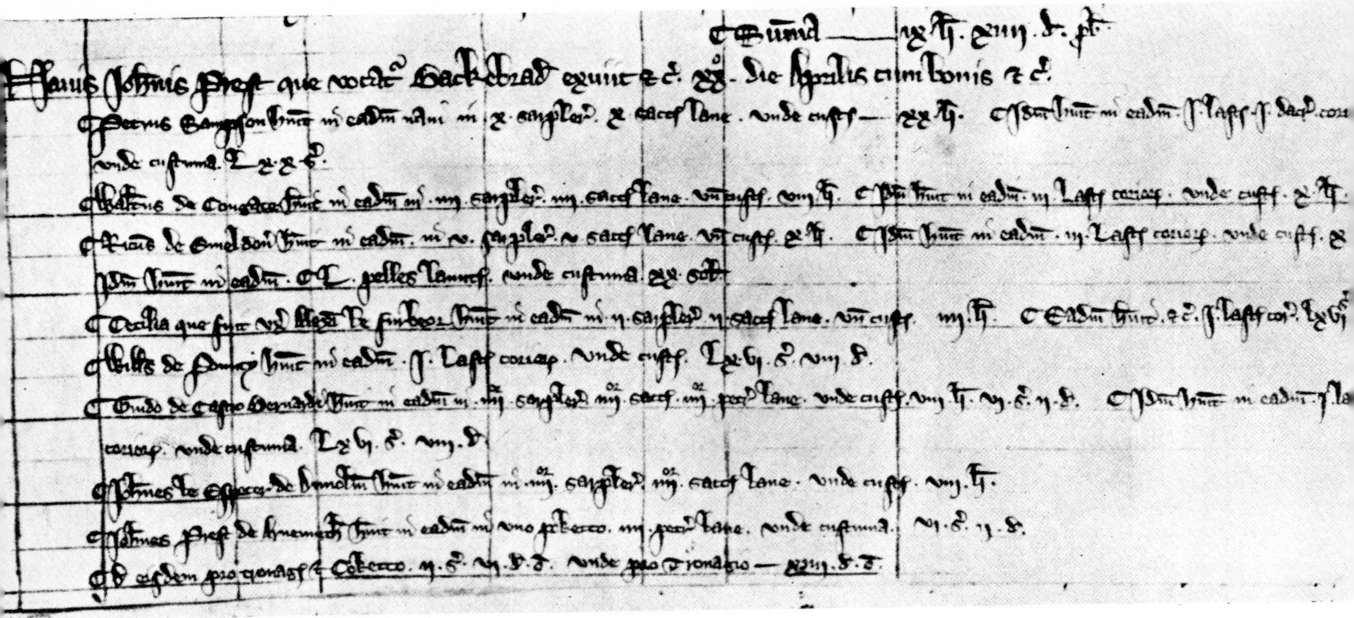

13. Newcastle Wool Customs Account for April 1297, recording the sailing of the *Backebrad*.

14. Alnmouth. A new town of the middle ages, carved out of Lesbury Common as an outport for Alnwick.

The 12th and 13th centuries were periods of great agricultural expansion in Northumberland as elsewhere in England. There was a growing population, strong Norman organisation, and an improving climate with better growing conditions. New arable land was broken in from the wastes and in some places entire new villages formed.

Breaking up new ground

The expansion of existing arable can be seen at Chirton on the south of the great Shire Moor that lasted in south-east Northumberland right through to the end of the 18th century. By a deed of 1320 Henry Fawkes of Backworth granted to Tynemouth Priory, 60 acres of Rodestane Moor north of Chirton to bring into cultivation. A 1250 survey reveals even larger intakes from the commons of Shoreston and North Sunderland near Bamburgh. The bondagers of Shoreston had recently broken in 18 new acres from the moor, and bondagers at North Sunderland 312 new acres. In the south of the county at Whittonstall, Hugh de Baliol in about 1200 granted 314 acres to be assarted (cleared of trees), cultivated, built upon and enclosed. This was probably the origin of Newlands village on the Ebchester road. Later another 200 acres were added.

About a mile north of Ashington, on the Ellington road, is the site of New Moor farm. The origin of this settlement was in a marriage agreement about 1160–80, when Hugh de Morwick was granted Ashington 'et territorium ad unam villam edificandam in Pendmor', land to build a village in Pendmoor. Pendmoor means Penda's swamp, and one can readily imagine the efforts to cultivate arable from the damp lands that still surround the Potland Burn today.

In the uplands the margins of farming were also being expanded, and many shielings became permanent settlements. In Tynedale, Dunclíueshalch, the site of one of the hunting lodges of William the Lion in about 1166, was by 1279 the settlement of Donkleywood with arable fields. By 1292 le Carrisideschel, by the Wark Burn, was a settlement with holdings of arable and meadow, as was Shiel Dyke on Alnwick Moor north of Newton-on-the-Moor.

New settlements were also carved out of the forests. The King's forest of Rothbury on the slopes of the Simonside hills was nibbled away by a whole series of clearings. Before 1200 the canons of Brinkburn paid the King 20 marks (a mark was 13s. 4d., or 67p), so that the 100 acres of assarts they had made in the forests might be free of all restraints, and a number of laymen also paid 16 marks for the same purpose. In 1204 Rothbury forest was granted to Robert Fitzroger, and the village of Newtown was created sometime between 1214 and 1242. By 1249 it had 270 acres of arable land. Pastureland was also important, and in 1249 the villagers of Rothbury paid 14s. (70p) a year so their animals could use the wood during the 'fence-month', when the wood was normally restricted to the deer. But these inroads into the hunting areas provoked landowners to create specific deer-parks to protect their game. Such parks were built at Warkworth, Acklington and Chillingham. Here in Rothbury forest, a deer park was created in 1275. Robert Fitzroger surrounded part of the forest with a stone wall, a section of which can still be seen on the slopes of the Simonsides near the small road from Lordenshaws to Tosson. Not surprisingly, the commoners reacted and at the 1279 Assize the Rothbury jurors complained that Robert had enclosed part of the forest they needed for their cattle. They added that Robert had bought off the local parson, giving him six acres as a park to stop him objecting.

The last decades of the 13th century saw the high water mark of this tide of agrarian expansion. Warfare with Scotland was about to destroy many of these gains. We, fortunately, possess a detailed tax assessment, taken in the last year of peace, 1296. This Lay Subsidy Roll is preserved in the Public Record Office. As a record it has many flaws, but it still gives, village by village, a unique assessment of relative wealth. Glendale, near the border over the Tweed, had the villages with the greatest average wealth. East and West Coquetdale, which included villages up to Lilburn and Chatton, was the second most wealthy. The heavy clay lands south of the Coquet were much poorer with Tynemouthshire at the bottom. So Monkseaton was assessed at only £18 7s. 2d. (£18.36p), whereas Thockrington, now an isolated farm near Sweethope Lough, was assessed at £41 5s. 9d. (£41.29p), and Hethpool, west of Wooler, at £48 16s. 2d. (£48.82p).

Thockrington church

VII The Anglo-Scottish Wars

The prosperity of 13th-century Northumberland was paralleled north of the border in Scotland. The royal burghs grew, trade expanded and agriculture flourished. The Southern Uplands were grazed by the sheep of the great monasteries, and their wool provided the trade for the important towns of Roxburgh and Berwick. Berwick was the greatest Scottish port, 'a second Alexandria', and in 1286 its customs revenue was over £2,000, compared with Newcastle's £323 in 1282.

There were close links between Northumberland and Scotland. The border was long established, but it separated two regions with much in common. Lothian had been part of Anglian Northumbria, and the 12th century had seen extensive Norman settlement in southern Scotland. There was much common landholding across the border: Gilbert de Umfraville, baron of Prudhoe, and holder of Redesdale, was also Earl of Angus. The Gospatric family, descendants of the old pre-Conquest Northumbrian royal house, were now Earls of Dunbar, but also held the Beanley barony in the Aln valley. The Scots' king himself held Tynedale.

This prosperity and accord was swept away after Alexander III of Scotland died in 1286. An early fragment of Scots' verse claimed that 'Qwhen Alexander our kynge was dede' then 'our golde was changit into lede', a backward look to a golden age that had more justice than such claims usually have. The King's successor was a very young child, Margaret of Norway. A group of Guardians took control of Scotland, and negotiated that the girl should eventually marry Edward I's son and heir. However, Margaret died on her way from Norway, and faced with rivals for the throne the Scots reluctantly allowed Edward to arbitrate. This he did, at the price of recognition of his overlordship of Scotland, and he decided in favour of John Balliol, who did homage to Edward.

As late as Michaelmas 1295 there was still peace on the border, and Ellen de Prenderlath, a Scotswoman, invested a legacy in a mortgage secured by a lease on Moneylaws, just on the English side of the Tweed. The Scots, however, had had enough of Edward I's claims to overlordship. In Berwick, English ships were burnt and merchants killed, and a group took Wark Castle. Edward rapidly recaptured Wark and besieged Berwick, which he took with great ferocity, slaughtering many of the inhabitants. In a counter-move

Warkworth Castle

Arms of Adam Swynburne

the same month, April 1296, a party of Scots, aided by Adam Swynburne of East Swynburne in Tynedale, raided across the Cheviots, burning villages and crops, damaging Hexham Priory, and, according to English propaganda that was probably a gross exaggeration or distortion, burning alive 200 schoolboys at Corbridge school.

This outbreak of war was to lead to 300 years of trouble and poverty along the border. Many landowners were torn in their loyalties, and several Northumbrians like Swynburne, Wishart of Moneylaws, and Ros of Wark sided with the Scots. Although William Wallace, a leader of the Scottish independence revolt, wasted much of the county in 1297 from a base in Rothbury forest (but was unsuccessful in besieging the castles), Edward I was largely victorious and carried the war into Scotland. But after Edward's death in 1307, Robert Bruce's campaign of 'defending himself with the longest stick he had' led to raids in Northumberland. In 1308 the crops at Temple Thornton near Netherwitton had been 'sold in a hurry through dread of a raid of the Scots'. The Community of Northumberland paid Bruce £2,000 in blackmail for truces in 1311 and 1312–13. Cattle and sheep were driven off, crops taken or destroyed. The discord of Edward II and his barons led to weak resistance; some, like Thomas of Lancaster, had dealings with Bruce.

After his defeat at Bannockburn in 1314, Edward still refused to recognise Scottish independence, so Bruce ran an intensified terror campaign in the north of England, penetrating as far as north Yorkshire. There was great devastation, but because it was remote from the heartland of southern England, Edward was slow to react. The record for Tarset in Redesdale in 1315 that 'the manor is now worth nothing because it lies waste and destroyed by the Scots' is repeated in village after village. The coalmines at Cullercoats were destroyed. Law and order collapsed, and the people were torn between the Scots and local oppressors like Jack le Irroys. In 1316 the inhabitants of Bamburgh complained that this constable of Bamburgh Castle refused to let them buy off Bruce for £270 unless they paid him an equal amount. There were many petitions for war damage, and in 1318 Edward ordered the distribution of 40 tuns of wine to deserving members of the Northumbrian gentry.

The disasters of these years were compounded by a wet summer and ruined harvest in 1315, and great famine the following year. In desperation at Edward's lack of protection for the county, a group of Northumbrian knights and gentry led by Sir Gilbert de Middleton rebelled in 1317, in alliance with the Scots and possibly with Lancaster. They kidnapped the Bishop-elect of Durham and two cardinals, and held Mitford and Horton Castles. The rebels were defeated, but, although they have often been pictured as mere bandits, the revolt was partly a response to the breakdown of law and order, and their action is understandable. Many Northumbrians changed sides at this time.

The English continued to refuse to agree to a treaty, and in 1327 Bruce led a further series of devasting raids. This time he may have planned to annex Northumberland, for he granted land charters to his followers, such as part of Belford to a member of the Scrymgeour family. The 'poure gentz de la Communaute de Northumbreland' petitioned Edward for pardon of war-time debts as 200 townships lay deserted. This time Edward did agree to a treaty, but with Bruce's death shortly after, Balliol renewed his claims, and there was a drift into regular war again.

It would serve no useful purpose to recount the detailed sequence of battles, raids and truces over the period 1330 to 1490. It is unlikely the devastation was ever as great as that in the period of Bruce's terror campaign, though that was, of course, the period when there was still something to lose. The 1330s saw the war carried into Scotland and the establishment of an English-controlled buffer region in south-east Scotland. But raids continued, and in 1346 David Bruce ravaged around Slaley and Blanchland before being defeated at Neville's Cross. After a truce of eight years there was war again in 1355, when Sir Thomas Gray was captured at the siege of Norham and imprisoned in Edinburgh, where he began his great chronicle of the border war, *Scalachronica.*

Another disaster magnified the tragedy of 14th-century Northumberland. In 1349 the Black Death or plague struck with even worse effect than the Scots. Many died, and the local economy was disrupted: at Monkseaton in the south-east, the bondage holdings were reduced by one-third, and as late as 1377 six of the other 10 farms had lain waste 'since the time of the first pestilence'. At Belford there were so many dead the gentry had to ask for a local cemetery as Bamburgh was too distant.

One aspect of the years 1330 to 1400 is particularly important: a change in the power structure in the county. Many of the older families were ruined by the Scots' raids or by confiscation following their choosing the wrong side at the wrong time. Power and influence increasingly went to holders of military and Crown office, with their incomes, military backing and acquisition of forfeited lands. Foremost were the Percies, an old-established family in Sussex and Yorkshire, but who had only acquired the Alnwick barony in 1309 from Bishop Bek. In 1331 they got Warkworth barony, and made Warkworth Castle their main home, and later acquired the Prudhoe barony from

Arms of Sir Henry Percy

Arms of Sir John Coupland

the Umfravilles, who largely retreated into their Lincolnshire lands. During the 14th century the Percies (who became Earls of Northumberland), along with the Nevilles, rose to be the main military and political leaders in the north, serving as Wardens of the Marches. A host of lesser men also rose in status through the wars, and this was highly resented by the older families, in one case at least leading to murder. John Coupland was a local man who had risen in the royal service, especially after capturing David Bruce at Neville's Cross. He was made a banneret with a £500 annuity and was several times sheriff of the county. (It is interesting to note that one of his fellow sheriffs in the 1350s was Alan del Strother, who was probably one of the two clerks celebrated in Chaucer's *Reeve's Tale*.) Coupland was murdered on Bolton Moor near Alnwick just before Christmas in 1363 by a group of Northumbrian gentry, a murder that was covered up by the investigating jury, not surprisingly since the jury contained Sir William Heron, one of the instigators of the murder.

The new men had come to say, however. Border warfare became institutionalised, with local leaders having a vested interest in its continuation, and in raiding and plunder. Even during formal truces there were private raids by both sides, often instigated by the great barons themselves. On the Scottish side the Douglases filled the role of the Percies and there was great rivalry between the families, culminating in the Scots' raid on Durham in 1388, the subsequent personal combat between Harry Hotspur and Douglas before the Walls of Newcastle, and the Scottish victory (but Douglas's death) at the battle of Otterburn. In 1402 the Percies got their revenge at the battle of Homildon Hill near Wooler. The power acquired by these great border magnates through their standing armies grew to be a threat to both the English and Scottish kings. The power of Percy and Neville put Bolinbroke on the throne in 1399, and these families were heavily involved in the English political conflicts of the 15th century. For a short period from 1461 to 1464 Northumberland was the focus of the Wars of the Roses, with Edward IV defeating the Lancastrians at Percy's Cross and Hexham, and besieging Bamburgh and Dunstanburgh. These conflicts, combined with internal political problems in Scotland, meant that there was less organised border warfare than in the 14th century. But this did not relieve the poverty or halt the intermittent fighting and raiding. So in 1416 Hepple in Coquetdale was destroyed by the Scots, and again in 1436, and in the late 1440s the Douglases burnt Alnwick and Warkworth. The future Pope, Aeneas Sylvius Piccolomini, travelled through Northumberland in 1435 and recorded a bleak picture. The houses were of earth or wood, white bread was unknown, and at night all the men took shelter from the Scots in a local pele-tower, but left the women outside, saying that they would not be harmed. Aeneas was glad to reach Newcastle and commented 'Northumberland was uninhabitable, horrible, uncultivated'.

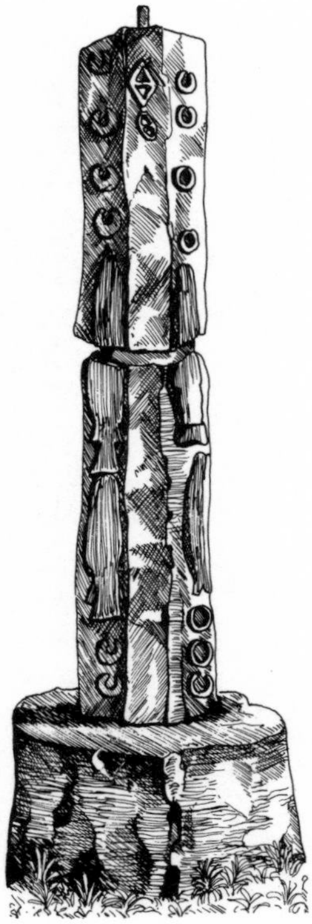

Percy's Cross, near Hedgeley Moor

VIII Churches and Monasteries

Tynemouth priory

In 1074, eight years after the Norman Conquest, three monks arrived at the banks of the Tyne, and a revival of monasticism in the North began. They were Aldwin, a monk from Winchcombe in Gloucestershire, with two companions from the Evesham monastery, and they had travelled on foot with a donkey to carry their vestments and books. They found the old monastery at Tynemouth to be uninhabitable, and were persuaded by the Bishop of Durham to settle at Jarrow.

In the succeeding years, other monastic communities were established: at Lindisfarne in 1082, as a cell of Durham; at Tynemouth in 1083; the Augustinians at Hexham in 1113, and at Brinkburn on the Coquet in 1135; the Cistercian order at Newminster in 1139, and the Premonstratensians at Alnwick in 1147, and Blanchland, on the Durham border, in 1165. Nunneries were set up at Holystone, during the reign of Alexander I of Scotland (1107–1124), and at Guyzance before 1147 (Plate 9). There was also a major rebuilding of churches. One of the finest and most complete is St. Lawrence's at Warkworth, built on the site of an earlier Anglo-Saxon church (Plate 11).

The foundation of the monasteries was only made possible because of large grants of land and money by the Norman nobility, and many of the monks were themselves men of rank and wealth. Brinkburn, for example, was established by William Bertram of Mitford, who gave the abbey large grants of land in mid-Coquetdale. Ralph de Gaugy, baron of Ellingham, gave the convent of Durham the endowment of Ellingham church, and this charter has survived intact (Plate 10). These grants established the monasteries as major landowners and economic forces. In addition, there were many smaller gifts: amongst hundreds of grants, Brinkburn received the wood on Rimside moor, a marl-pit at Weldon, a marsh below the spring in Old Felton, licence to buy and sell in Alnwick, a shop in Corbridge, and a saltpan in Warkworth.

The Church grew to wield great political power. In the North-east the Bishopric of Durham was very powerful, especially under Bishops like Antony Bek (Bishop 1283–1311) and Thomas Langley (1406–1437), both of whom were high officials of the King. At the beginning of the Scottish troubles, Bishop Bek, a close adviser of Edward I, acquired control of Tynedale, Penrith in Cumberland,

15. The Keep, Newcastle Upon Tyne. Built in 1168-1179 by Henry III. The present battlements are early 19th century additions.

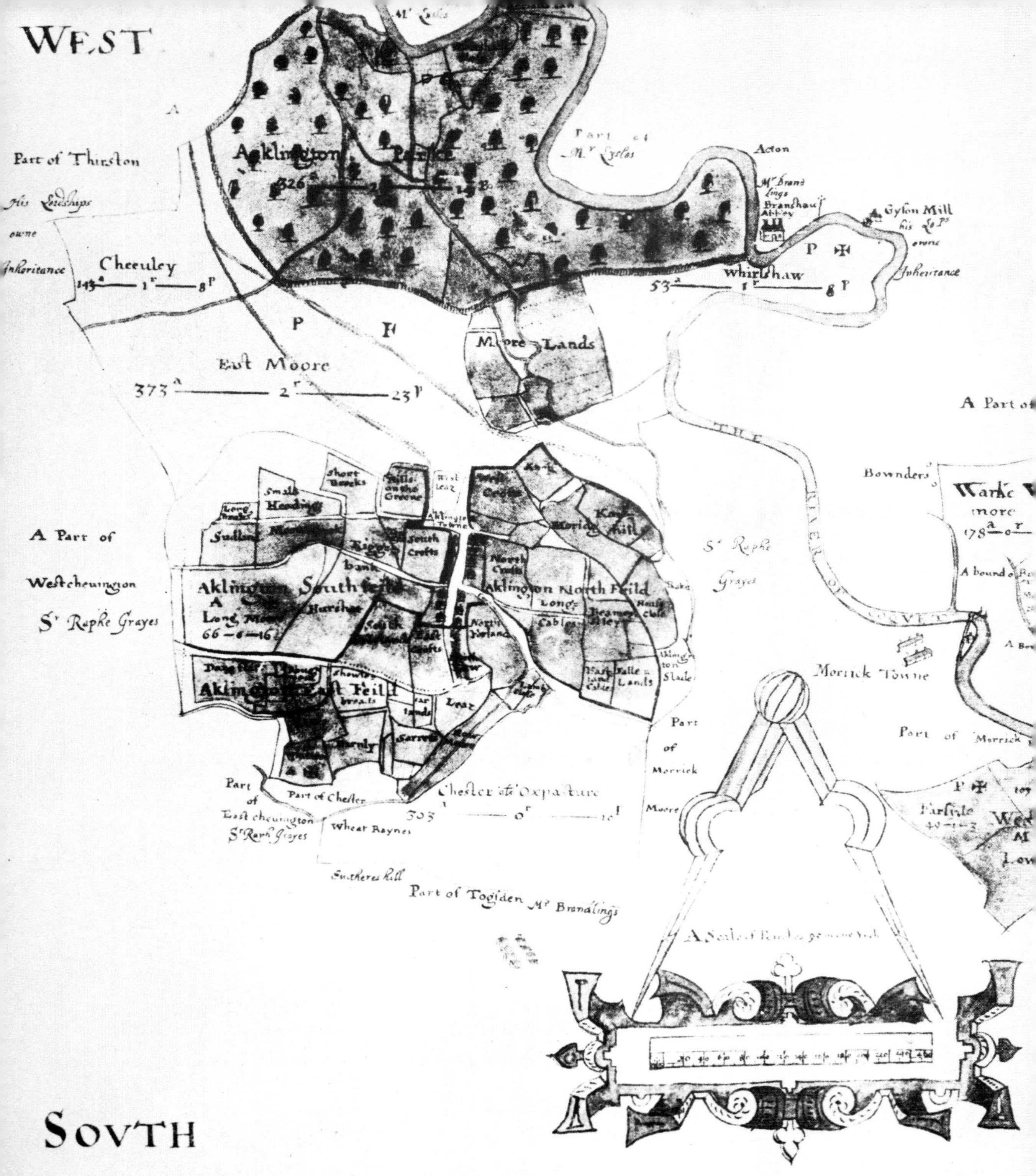

16. Acklington Park and Common Fields in 1616, depicted on a Percy estate surveyor's map.

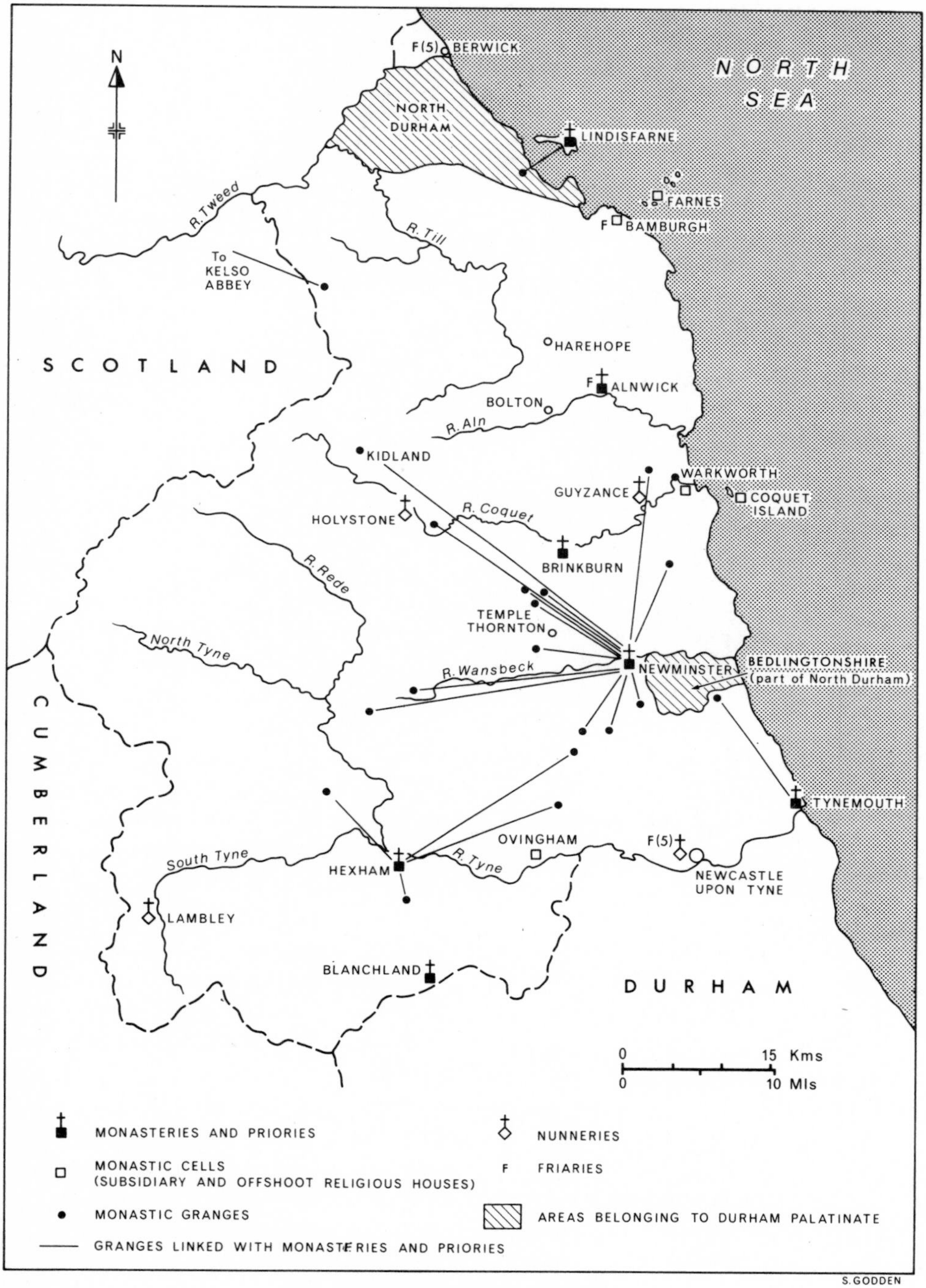
NORTH SEA
BERWICK
F(5)
NORTH DURHAM
LINDISFARNE
FARNES
F BAMBURGH
R. Tweed
R. Till
To KELSO ABBEY
SCOTLAND
HAREHOPE
F ALNWICK
BOLTON
R. Aln
KIDLAND
WARKWORTH
COQUET ISLAND
GUYZANCE
HOLYSTONE
R. Coquet
BRINKBURN
R. Rede
TEMPLE THORNTON
North Tyne
NEWMINSTER
BEDLINGTONSHIRE (part of North Durham)
R. Wansbeck
CUMBERLAND
TYNEMOUTH
OVINGHAM
F(5)
South Tyne
HEXHAM
R. Tyne
NEWCASTLE UPON TYNE
LAMBLEY
BLANCHLAND
DURHAM
0 15 Kms
0 10 Mls
MONASTERIES AND PRIORIES
NUNNERIES
MONASTIC CELLS (SUBSIDIARY AND OFFSHOOT RELIGIOUS HOUSES)
F FRIARIES
MONASTIC GRANGES
AREAS BELONGING TO DURHAM PALATINATE
GRANGES LINKED WITH MONASTERIES AND PRIORIES
S.GODDEN

5. Monastic Northumberland

Arms of Bishop Bek

the Isle of Man, the Vesci barony of Alnwick and its related estates, and the barony of Langley in Allendale. These lands, together with the traditional Bishopric lands in Durham and Northumberland, created a virtual cordon across the North. Bek, however, fell foul of his patron, and the new acquisitions were either confiscated or sold off.

The increasing wealth and political power of the Church caused many to consider the Church was being corrupted from Christ's teaching, and from this belief arose the various orders of friars, vowed to live in poverty and to help the poor. They lived mainly in the towns. The Carmelites founded friaries at Hulne (Alnwick) in 1242, and at Berwick and Newcastle. The Dominicans settled at Bamburgh and Newcastle, and the Franciscans at Berwick and Newcastle. Over the years these groups also tended to acquire wealth. Hospitals were also established, some as hostels for travellers. At Bolton, near Edlingham, Robert de Ros founded a leper hospital in 1225 for a master, three chaplains and 13 lepers, and at nearby Harehope another leper hospital, run by the order of St. Lazarus, was started in 1247.

The monasteries were major contributors to the medieval expansion of cultivation and land use. The Cistercians of Newminster, as was typical of their order, were particularly active in this, running outlying farms or granges right across mid-Northumberland from Sturton Grange on Warkworth Moor to Wreighill in upper Coquetdale. They brought extensive upland areas into use as sheep-grazing, particularly in Kidland and Cheviot. They first got a lease of Kidland from Odinell de Umfraville in 1181, though he kept his hunting rights and insisted that the monks' dogs had one foot cut off to prevent their chasing the game. By 1270 the abbey was able to sell Jehan Boinebroke 72 sacks of its own wool and 20 sacks of collected wool, which add up to at least 18,000 fleeces. Other monasteries, such as Tynemouth and Lindisfarne, also had granges for pasture or grain-production. On Lindisfarne the Prior's accounts reveal the careful farming. The oxen were muzzled as they led the corn from the harvested field, in case the animals should chew the bound sheaves. Women were hired to weed the thistles from the wheat fields, and these thistles, after softening in the sun, then provided fodder for the horses. The expanding margin of cultivation can be seen in numerous examples: about 1225 Roger Bertram gave the Holystone nuns his wood of Baldwineswood, which they 'ridded' or assarted, creating Nunriding, west of Mitford, still held by the nuns at the Dissolution of the monasteries and rented out at £1 6s. 8d. (£1.33p) a year. In 1234 the brethren of Bolton hospital got a grant to enclose the 120 acres they had broken in from the moor and the 150 acres they had cleared from wood.

The disasters of the 14th century seriously affected the religious houses. The Scottish Wars took their toll, both on the lands and income of the monasteries and churches, and also on life and limb in frontier areas. The nunnery of Holystone, high up in the lower folds of the Cheviots, had to be abandoned during the summer raids of the Scots in 1322, and in August Edward II, as he passed through Newcastle, gave alms to the nuns who had fled there. Ten years later the nuns were granted 10 quarters of wheat from the royal stores at Newcastle because their corn and granges had been burnt and their cattle driven off by the Scots. The Black Death of 1349 also struck communal institutions hard, and many smaller foundations became extinct during the century. The nunnery of Guyzance is not heard of after 1313.

The religious life never fully recovered from these disasters. Numbers fell: Holystone had 27 nuns in 1313, but only eight in 1432. Society became less well disposed towards them, and gifts declined during the 15th century. Tynemouth received no lands after 1404. The small legacies to all the religious houses in the North-east given in Roger Thornton's will in 1429, which brought Holystone one fother of lead, were amongst the last of their type. The worldly preoccupation of the religious houses became more obvious: the major priors and abbots were border lords, and the abbeys regarded as sources of food and supplies by the military and political leaders.

The decline continued in the first half of the 16th century. At Alnwick there were 25 canons in 1500, but only 17 on the pension list after the Dissolution. At Blanchland at the beginning of the century, the abbot could not even find a barber and washerwoman for the community. Henry VIII's decision to suppress the monasteries did not therefore destroy a thriving institution. In 1536 his Commissioners dissolved all houses with less than £200 income, and in 1538 and 1539 the larger monasteries. After the first suppressions, there were desperate attempts by the larger houses to prolong their lives. At Tynemouth they tried to get the support of influential landowners by granting them long leases on monastic lands: in September 1536 Thomas Lawson of Cramlington was granted a 41-year lease on Hartford, and in October Robert Collingwood got a 61-year lease of Bewick. But it was to no avail.

The only attempts at resistance were at Newminster (where a mob from Morpeth razed the abbey to the ground) and Hexham. Although its income was slightly over £200 Hexham was included

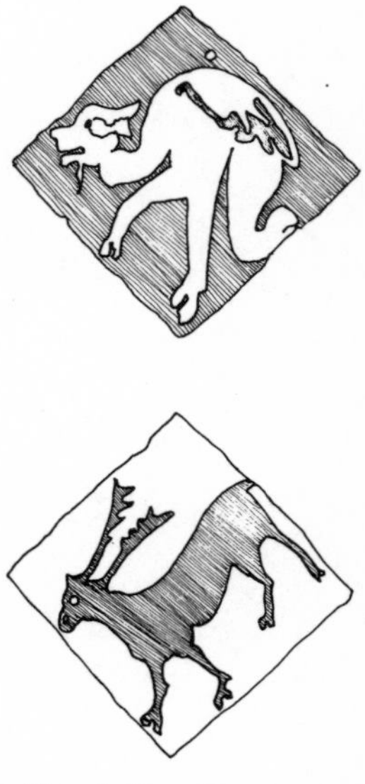

Medieval tiles, Newminster

in the 1536 suppressions, but the canons refused to open the gates and when the Commissioners arrived in September, the Master of the cell of Ovingham appeared above the gateway in armour. The canons were encouraged by some of the local gentry, and the resistance became a very minor part of the Pilgrimage of Grace, a general revolt by northern leaders against not just religious reform, but also the growing centralisation of power in royal hands. When the movement collapsed (in Northumberland it had been mainly an occasion for inter-family feuding), the canons ceased their resistance.

The impact of the Dissolution was felt in several ways. Effects on the land market are explored later. The religious were dispossessed. It is important to get their numbers in proportion. Despite the vast estates they controlled, the total number of religious in Northumberland and Newcastle affected was only about 230 people. These were pensioned and most were absorbed into the parish church system. Some, such as the Premonstratensians at Alnwick, had already been sending monks into parishes for some time. After 1538 William Hudson became master of Alnwick grammar school, Robert Blake was a chantry priest at St. Nicholas', Newcastle, and Robert Forster a curate at Alnmouth. The former prior of Tynemouth, Robert Blakeney, farmed his manor of Benwell, and John Gray of the Austin friars at Newcastle became vicar of Chillingham. The nuns, mostly from wealthy families, returned to them. In the case of Agnes Lawson, prioress of the Benedictine nunnery in Newcastle, her family bought up the nunnery and lands.

Medieval stained glass, St. Nicholas's, Newcastle

IX Medieval Merchants, Towns and Trade

The agrarian expansion of medieval Northumberland was accompanied by a parallel growth in both regional exports and internal trade. The county's grain produce was mainly for local consumption, and the main exports came from pastoral activity: the hides of cattle and the wool of sheep. In medieval England such trade was not carried on in a free market, but was strictly regulated: rights to sell and trade were monopolies and privileges granted by royal and baronial charters, usually in return for higher rents and taxes. At least as early as the mid-12th century Newcastle established its rights for the export of hides, wool and woolfells (wool on the skin) from the region. The internal history of the town and its charters will be studied in Chapter X. In accounts for about 1290, Newcastle headed the list of English ports for the export of leather. At this time the export of wool was growing in importance, and Edward I's decision to raise money by customs dues on wool and hides meant detailed records of many of these exports were kept and have survived. Northern wool was coarse and of poor quality compared with the best English fleeces. In 1337 it sold at five marks a sack (about 26 stones), against Herefordshire's 12 marks and Shropshire's ten. But although it had to pay customs dues at the same rate, it was still a profitable export. In the early 14th century Newcastle ranked sixth in English wool exports. There had been a notable expansion during Edward's reign: for Easter 1292–93, Newcastle exported 841 sacks of wool, 8,042 woolfells and 55 lasts of hides (a last was 200 hides). By 1304–5 the trade was 1910 sacks of wool and 35,000 woolfells.

From the customs accounts we can see the details of the trade. Plate 13 shows the customs entry for the sailing of John Prest's ship the *Backebrad* on 20 April 1297. The captain took some wool on his own account, but his cargo included about 20 sacks for Peter Sampson (line 2), eight for Richard of Embleton, and eight for Walter of Cowgate. The main destinations at this time were the clothmakers of Flanders. Already the exporting and shipping businesses were becoming separate, and many of the ships were foreign. In a seven-year period, out of 205 sailings from Newcastle, 170 were sailings of 162 foreign ships, the vast majority making a single journey. Twenty-two came from Middleburg, 17 from Calais, 13 from St. Valery, and 12 from Barfleur, though a few single sailings went to northerly ports like

14th-century merchant ship

Arms of Peter Graper

Groningen and Lubeck. The ships themselves were mostly very small, less than 100 tons, and smaller than North Sea drifters. The export trade itself was largely in English and local hands. Out of 216 merchants who traded through Newcastle in the same seven years, 138 were foreign (mainly from Flanders), but they made mostly small, single shipments. Seven belonged to the Italian trading societies, and these ran larger shipments, such as James Clare of Florence, who exported 87½ sacks between 1287 and 1293 for the Society of the White Circles, and Villan Iscoldi, representative of the Black Circles, exported 52 sacks in 1297. The bulk was handled, however, by the English merchants, especially the 50 based in Newcastle.

In the 1296 Subsidy we can identify the major traders. The richest individual was Samson le Cutiller, assessed at £53 14s. 4s. (£53.72p), who paid more tax than whole groups of villages in the county. (By comparison, Sir Richard Craster, a typical county knight, was assessed at £10 4s. 8d. [£10.23p].) Hugh Gerardin and Isolda de Pampeden (Pandon) were jointly assessed at £84 in St. Nicholas's parish. Gerardin shipped 110 sacks and 520 woolfells in 1293–96. Other important merchants were Peter Graper, exporting 103 sacks in 1292–97, Peter Sampson with 77 sacks in the 1290s, and Adam of Hoga who was based in Wooler. In 1308 Richard of Embleton was personally responsible for an eighth of the town's exports.

If customs were paid at Newcastle, the wool could actually be shipped from another northern port. In July 1292 James Clare paid dues on 16 sacks of wool, which were carted at Alnwick three days later and shipped from Berwick. The proximity of the Scottish border encouraged smuggling. The Scottish port of Berwick had lower dues, and when it was in English hands in 1340 Newcastle burgesses complained that Northumbrian wool was being sent north to pay only half a mark a sack, instead of three at Newcastle. Smuggling was also encouraged by the staple port system which was introduced in 1313 to ease customs collections. All wool exports had to be channelled through certain ports, sometimes a group of home ports, sometimes Continental ports. Newcastle often got exemption from the system, but whenever exports were forced to go through a port like Calais, Newcastle's trade (which was mainly with markets further north) became much more costly. Many prominent merchants smuggled, even the customs officers. In 1341–42 William de Acton was fined 200 marks for exporting 14 sacks of uncustomed wool, and John of Denton 250 marks, and in 1364 a group chartered the *Katherine* to take coal from Newcastle, but in fact loaded it with 16 sacks of wool and 600 woolfells for uncustomed export to Zeeland.

The Scottish wars had a major influence on trade. The hide and wool trades were disrupted, shipping became more hazardous, and special taxes were demanded to fund the war. But war-contracts could also be lucrative for some merchants, and in 1332 John of Denton provided 393 quarters of wheat, 202 of oats, and 22 tuns of wine for the King's forces. Although wool remained the major export, Newcastle merchants exploited commodities found in the immediate vicinity, and so less liable to disruption. Grindstones from the Gateshead Fells were a standard export down to the 18th century, giving rise to the 17th-century saying that 'three things were to be found the world over—a Scot, a rat, and a Newcastle grindstone'. Coal from local mines became a significant trade commodity (see Chapter XIII), though it was not dominant until the 16th century. A trade balance for 1508–9 constructed by I. S. W. Blanchard values the coal trade at £225, but wool at £498. Lead exports, mainly from Weardale, had grown to £267 worth.

The medieval trading pattern ended in the early 16th century, with the collapse of the cloth-trade in the West Brabant towns, Newcastle's main wool market, in the 1520s. Home cloth production in England was also taking much of the wool. In its place came the coal trade, and also an expansion of the Baltic or Eastland trade. Newcastle had a long history of trade with the Baltic, but for a long time it had been mainly carried in ships of the Hanseatic league of cities, who excluded English ships from the Baltic. In the 1390s there had been a brief English breakthrough, and in 1394 the cargo and crew of the *Good Year,* owned by Roger Thornton and others of Newcastle, were seized by the Hanseatic towns of Wismar and Rostock in a dispute over customs dues. The cargo of cloth and wine was valued at 200 marks. In the 16th century the Danish Sound was re-opened to English ships and, in 1537, 52 Newcastle ships entered the Baltic.

The Tyne's imports were much more diversified than the exports. In 1336 Richard Galloway, Robert de Shilvington and Adam Tredflour loaded the *Petit Cuthbert* of Newcastle at St. Valery-sur-Somme in France with cob-nuts, herring, cockles, 'blandurer' apples, woad, a carpet and a coverlet. From the Baltic came wooden boards, furs and corn. Wine imports, especially for Durham Priory, were important, and merchants like Robert de Castro acted as the Prior's agents.

Behind the regional exports and imports lay a network of internal trade and markets. Newcastle again dominated the scene, but at a local level there were many regular markets and fairs spread across the county, each usually based on a baronial administrative centre. So in 1257 Henry III confirmed to Roger de Merlay a Friday market at Netherwitton and a yearly fair of eight days on the eve, during and

Market cross, Alnwick

six days after St. Lawrence's Day (10 August), unless the market or fair were 'hurtful to neighbouring markets and fairs'. At the markets tolls were charged on many of the commodities, enabling us to identify the significant items. Grain was sold at most markets. Exotic groceries like pepper, cinnamon, almonds and figs appear in the accounts at Berwick, Newbiggin and Newcastle. Corbridge was the centre for ironware, selling horse-shoes by the thousand and nails by the two thousand. It also held the great cattle fair on Stagshawbank on Old Midsummer day (24 June). The record of an interesting transaction here in 1298 has survived. Robert of Hepple and John of Ireland bought up 72 oxen, ironware and wagons, probably to supply Edward I's army, but they purchased around the fair in small lots through many different agents so that news should not get out that there was a single big purchase on.

Between these regular markets and the great regional centre of Newcastle were a number of urban centres or burghs, distinguished from the surrounding countryside by their special rights and tenures. Like Newcastle, these centres gained or were granted privileges (e.g., freedom from market tolls and from labour services) by the King or local barons in return for taxes and rents. The old Anglo-Saxon burghs had been purely administrative centres, and several were in decline by the 13th century: Newburn is last heard of as a burgh in 1201, and in 1296 Rothbury was taxed at the rural rate. Corbridge, however, was the second town in Northumberland, with a population of about 1,500 people. Just as the agrarian expansion saw the creation of new villages in the Northumbrian landscape, so the commercial expansion led to the creation of 'new towns' and the planned expansion of old settlements. The incentive for the King or feudal lord was the increased rents from burgage property, tolls on market sales to outsiders, the presence of local craftsmen and general improvement of his estate. The King also charged higher taxes on borough wealth: in the 1296 Subsidy villagers paid one-eleventh of their assessed wealth, but burgesses paid one-seventh. Many of these local trading monopolies lasted a long time. Alnwick got a charter in 1157-85, and as late as 1735 the Merchants' Company of Alnwick voted that 'John Boulton of Warkworth be proceeded against for frequenting Alnwick market and selling lint'. At Morpeth a charter of the de Merlays gave Newminster monastery a piece of land 'ad capud novae villae de Morpath quam fundavi', 'to the top of the new town of Morpeth which I founded'. Hexham was expanded as centre of the York archbishopric's lands in the county. At Warkworth the main burgh, like others at Norham and elsewhere, was probably not intended as an urban centre, but rather as a rural settlement with

Moot Hall, Hexham

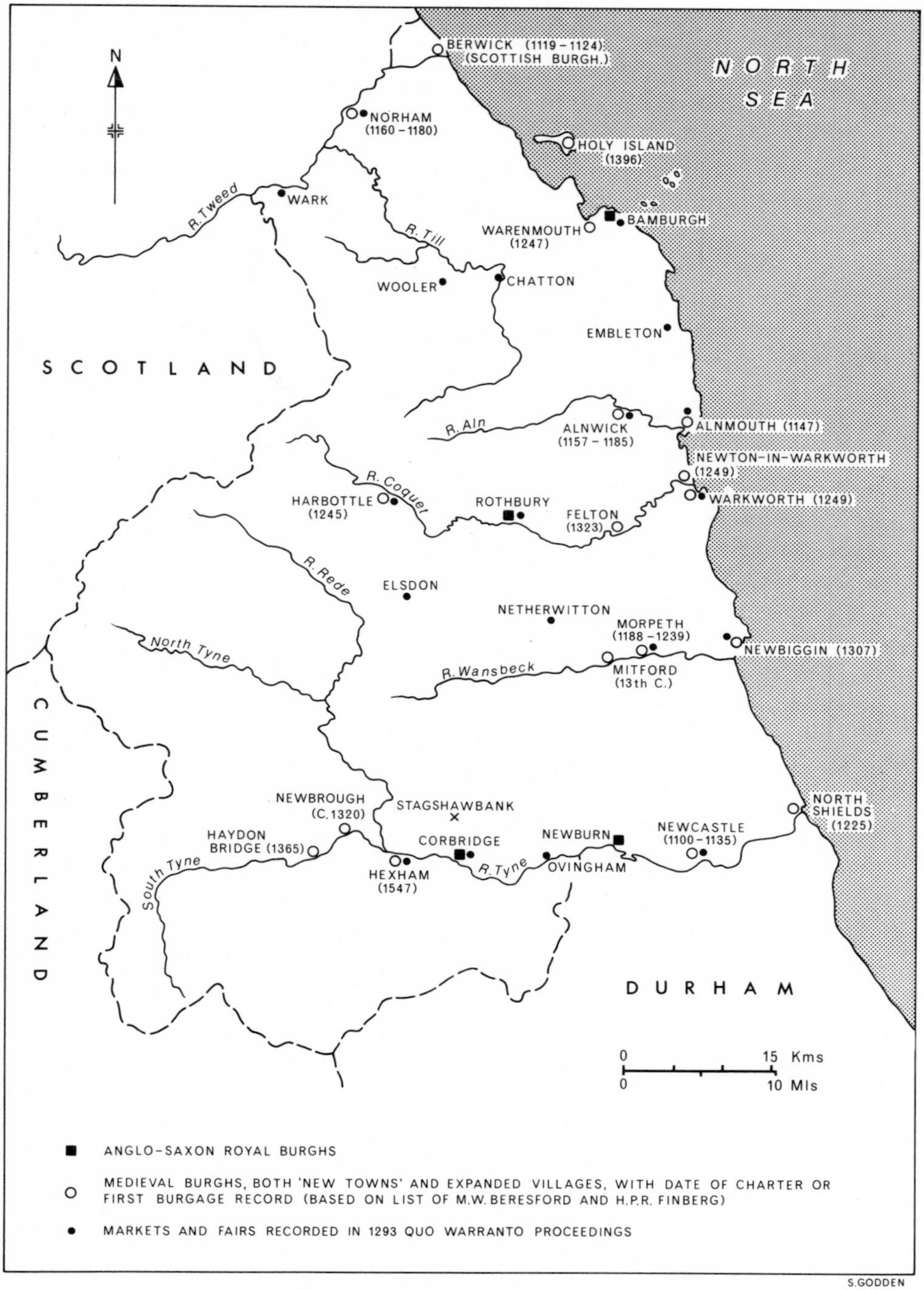
N
BERWICK (1119 – 1124) (SCOTTISH BURGH.)
NORTH SEA
NORHAM (1160 – 1180)
HOLY ISLAND (1396)
R. Tweed
WARK
R. Till
WARENMOUTH (1247)
BAMBURGH
WOOLER
CHATTON
EMBLETON
SCOTLAND
R. Aln
ALNWICK (1157 – 1185)
ALNMOUTH (1147)
NEWTON-IN-WARKWORTH (1249)
R. Coquet
HARBOTTLE (1245)
ROTHBURY
FELTON (1323)
WARKWORTH (1249)
R. Rede
ELSDON
NETHERWITTON
MORPETH (1188 – 1239)
NEWBIGGIN (1307)
North Tyne
R. Wansbeck
MITFORD (13th C.)
CUMBERLAND
NEWBROUGH (C. 1320)
STAGSHAWBANK
NORTH SHIELDS (1225)
NEWCASTLE (1100 – 1135)
HAYDON BRIDGE (1365)
CORBRIDGE
NEWBURN
South Tyne
HEXHAM (1547)
R. Tyne
OVINGHAM
DURHAM
0 15 Kms
0 10 Mls
ANGLO-SAXON ROYAL BURGHS
MEDIEVAL BURGHS, BOTH 'NEW TOWNS' AND EXPANDED VILLAGES, WITH DATE OF CHARTER OR FIRST BURGAGE RECORD (BASED ON LIST OF M.W. BERESFORD AND H.P.R. FINBERG)
MARKETS AND FAIRS RECORDED IN 1293 QUO WARRANTO PROCEEDINGS
S.GODDEN

6. Medieval Towns and Markets

Hotspur Gate, Alnwick

more tenurial and personal freedom than the normal countryside, in return for providing craftsmen and services for the baronial centre.

The difficulties of medieval road travel meant coastal trade was important and several of the new burghs were ports. At Warenmouth, near Bamburgh, William Heron got a grant in 1257 of all the liberties of Newcastle for his proposed new town, probably intended as a port for Bamburgh. At Alnmouth there was a 'burgh of St. Waleric' established by 1147 as an outport for Alnwick, and separately represented before the 1256 Assizes, where cases indicated tanning, stone exports and wine imports. In 1296 it was assessed at more than Morpeth. The plan of Alnmouth today still shows the planned burgage settlement carved out of Lesbury Common (Plate 14). At North Shields the Prior of Tynemouth tried to create a port, and by 1290 it was reported there were quays, bakeries, breweries, and about 100 houses. It was a good site, especially with the increasing silting of the Tyne up river, but it naturally came into conflict with the claims of the Newcastle burgesses to a monopoly over the whole tidal river. As Dr. Constance Fraser has commented: 'the advantages and disadvantages of restriction on trading facilities must have been the constant preoccupation of the 14th-century merchant–liberty for himself and restriction for his rivals'. In 1290 petition and counter-petition were made in Parliament by the Newcastle burgesses and the Prior; Newcastle won, largely by suggesting to Edward I that he might lose customs dues, and North Shields was suppressed, though it re-established itself after 1390.

Many of the medieval new towns failed. Already by 1296 Warenmouth's few taxpayers paid at the rural rate, and by the 16th century its very site was forgotten, though its legal status continued until it was dug out of the law books for final burial in the 1835 Municipal Corporations Act. On the north side of the river at Warkworth the 'novus villa' or Newton mentioned in 1249 never succeeded as a fishing port, though the regular lines of the burgage layout can still be traced today. Other towns suffered through the economic decline of the 14th-century and the Scottish wars.

X Medieval Newcastle

Medieval Newcastle begins with the building of the royal castle by William I's son, Robert, in 1080. There is no evidence of any earlier village around the site of the castle, although there were Anglo-Saxon settlements in the vicinity of Pandon and Monkchester (possibly around St. Andrew's church). The castle, of the motte-and-bailey type, was made of wood and earth, and the present stone Keep and castle walls were built between 1168 and 1179 (Plate 15). Around this fortress and the bridge built across the Tyne, on the line of the present Swing Bridge, there rapidly grew up a flourishing trading community and town.

Black Gate, the Castle, Newcastle

The importance of legal privileges in medieval trading has already been noted, and Newcastle's rapid growth was as much due to its gaining trading monopolies and efficiently enforcing them as to its location, port facilities and commercial enterprise. The 'Laws of Newcastle', dating from 1100–1139, are the earliest evidence of these gains. The oldest surviving copy is a manuscript only 11 inches by three-and-a-half inches, to be found in the Public Record Office in London. It records and confirms the rights of the Newcastle burgesses: 'No merchant, unless he be a burgess may buy (outside) the town either wool or leather or other merchandise, nor within the the borough except (of) burgesses', and 'No one but a burgess may buy webs (cloth) to dye, nor make nor cut them', together with other regulations, such as 'If a plea arise between a burgess and a merchant, it shall be concluded before the third ebb of the tide', and 'If a ship have put in at Tynemouth and wishes to depart, the burgesses may buy what they will'.

The medieval town grew up mainly on the higher ground to the north of the Castle, with the markets around St. Nicholas's church in the present Groat and Bigg markets, though buildings followed The Side down the steep descent to the bridge and marshy shore of the river. Growth to the east was restricted by the steep ravines of two small rivers no longer visible. The Lort Burn rose in the Leazes and descended down the line of Grey Street and Dean Street, entering the Tyne at the Sandhill, then an unreclaimed margin of the river. Further east Pandon Burn ran down from Barras Bridge to enter the Tyne at the east end of the present Quayside. The topographic problems faced by medieval Newcastle can only be recaptured today by walking the

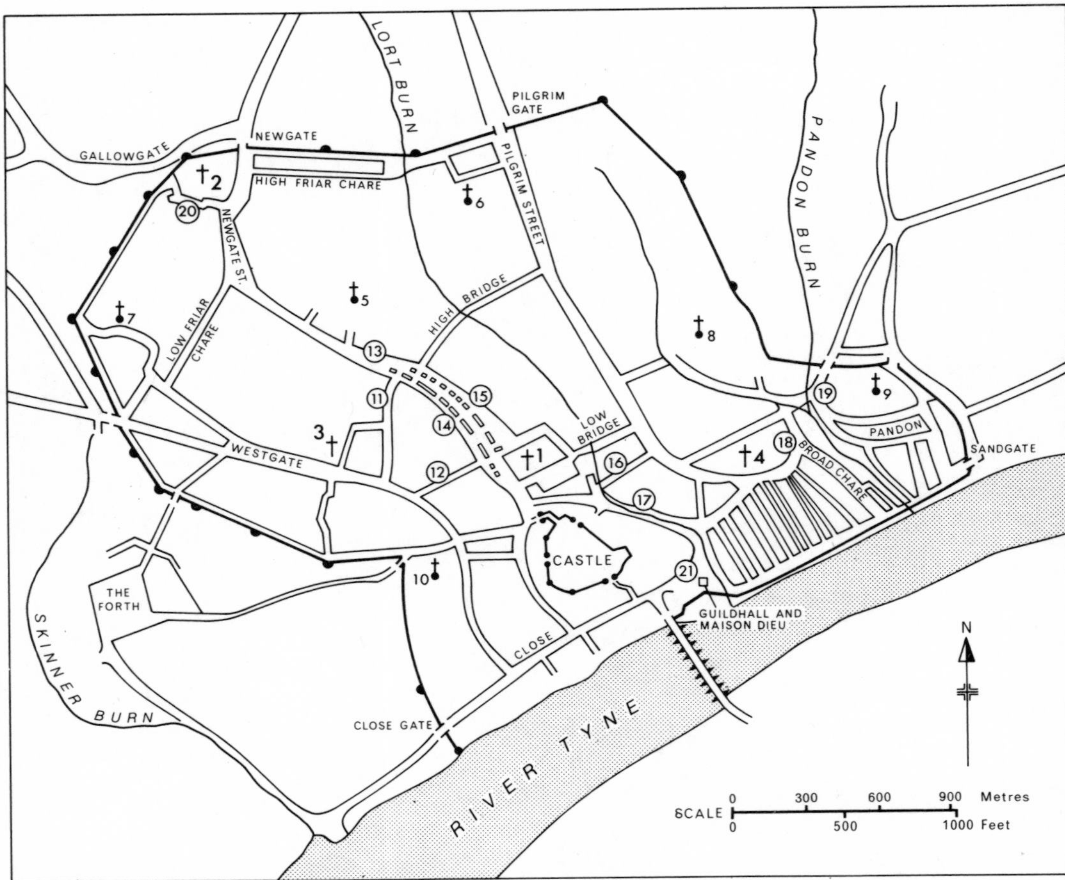

MEDIEVAL NEWCASTLE UPON TYNE

† CHURCHES

1 ST. NICHOLAS
2 ST. ANDREW
3 ST. JOHN
4 ALL HALLOWS (All Saints)

RELIGIOUS HOUSES

5 ST. BARTHOLOMEWS NUNNERY
6 FRANCISCAN FRIARS (GREYFRIARS)
7 DOMINICAN FRIARS (BLACKFRIARS)
8 AUSTIN FRIARS
9 CARMELITE FRIARS (Until 1307) WHITE FRIARS
10 CARMELITES (After 1307)

STREETS

11 PUDDING CHARE
12 DENTON CHARE
13 BIGG MARKET
14 GROAT MARKET
15 FLESH MARKET
16 PAINTER HEUGH
17 THE SIDE
18 COWGATE
19 STOCKBRIDGE
20 DARN CROOK
21 SANDHILL

S. GODDEN

old town on foot. Early growth was confined to the west side of the Lort Burn. By 1175 Westgate was a main street, and around St. Andrew's church Newgate Street was growing.

During the 13th century the town expanded rapidly. In 1220 a new parish of St. John's, Westgate, was carved out of the existing St. Nicholas's and St. Andrew's parishes, and by 1290 there was a continuous line of properties from St. Andrew's through the Bigg Market to St. Nicholas's. St. Bartholomew's nunnery had been established beside this road in the 12th century, and in the 13th century a number of friaries came to Newcastle: the Dominicans (1261), Franciscans (1274), Carmelites (1278), and Austins (1290). The Vicas Peregrinorum or Pilgrim Street, running down the east bank of the Lort Burn from the Franciscan friary to All Hallows (as All Saints was then known) and the Sandhill, is first mentioned in the 13th century. Between this street and the main markets around St. Nicholas's, two paths crossed the Lort Burn at High Bridge and Low Bridge, still to be found today. Lower down, almost at The Side, the Painter Heugh (now a derelict alley off Dean Street) went down from Pilgrim Street to the Lort, and is mentioned in 1373. Historians such as Bourne assure us that the river ebbed and flowed as far as Low Bridge and even High Bridge. Certainly the lower parts of the Lort Burn to the foot of The Side were navigable. By 1337 though, the Sandhill was being reclaimed from the river, for there were building plots on it, and in 1393 a royal proclamation cleared the Sandhill of stalls and merchandise for use as an open space. It was on the Sandhill that several of the noblemen on the wrong side at the Battle of Hexham in 1464 were beheaded.

Medieval Maison Dieu, Sandhill, in 1832

East of the town was the industrial village of Pandon, where fullers, dyers and brewers lived. In 1269–70 a fuller called John le Surays lived in Crosswellgate (now Pandon Street), and in 1278 the inhabitants petitioned the King because the Carmelite friars were monopolising Crosswell spring, which the dyers and fullers needed for their trade, and the merchants and sailors for drinking. The Pandon burn was crossed by Stockbridge, and this and Cowgate recall the location of the town's byres for the cows grazed on the Town Moor. Although much of Newcastle's trade was carried in foreign ships, there was clearly a small shipbuilding industry in the town, for in 1294 Newcastle was one of the ports ordered to build a galley for Edward I's fleet. The records of the galley's construction indicate that the vessel, designed to take up to 120 oars, was probably built in Pandon, and certainly docked there after being damaged during 'trials' up the coast to Bamburgh. In 1299 Newcastle formally annexed the suburb of Pandon. Between the Sandhill and Pandon, below All Hallows church, the Quayside was gradually being reclaimed from the river, and the dense, narrow lanes or chares began to be built. These were, however, very liable to flooding and in Edward III's reign 140 houses at the Pandon end were destroyed, and about 67 people drowned. As the port grew the areas around the Sandhill and Quayside, the lower town, became more important in the late middle ages.

Crown and spire of St. Nicholas's

The growth of the town was reflected in its ranking fourth in wealth in 1334, behind London, Bristol and York. After the plague the 1377 poll tax ranked it twelfth, with 2,647 taxpayers. An indication of its status is that Henry III had set up a mint in the town in 1249. Walls for the expanded town were begun about 1265, when a special murage toll was imposed on trade. The Newgate wall and stretch to the south west were built by 1285, and in the south east the wall had to be re-directed to encompass Pandon. The final curtain wall, over two miles long with seven gateways, 19 towers and 30 turrets, was not completed until after 1318, but the impetus of the Scottish wars forced the townsmen to complete the outer ditch or King's Dykes a few years earlier. Around Newgate this ditch could be flooded. Along the Quayside the wall ran from Sandgate to the Sandhill, with 17 watergates giving access to the river.

As the town and its commerce expanded, so it began to press for some municipal independence. During the 12th century the town was controlled by a royal bailiff, but in 1170 and 1213 it managed to negotiate some financial and judicial independence in exchange for annual payments to the King, set at £100 after 1213. Daniel, son of Nicholas, was chief bailiff in 1216 and is usually regarded as the first mayor, though royal approval for the title only came in 1251. We know nothing of the selection procedure for the mayor, but both the office and the town were controlled by the leading merchants. Until 1300 two families, the Scots and Carliols, monopolised the office, but after 1300 a number of the other leading wool merchants appear, such as Peter Graper, Richard Acton, John Denton, Richard Galloway, and Robert Angerton. Richard of Embleton held the office 23 times between 1305 and 1332.

Under the 'Laws of Newcastle' there were no legal or trading distinctions amongst the burgesses. However, in 1216 King John had allowed the formation of a merchant guild in Newcastle, and the leading exporters and importers began to gain control of all trading as well as politics. In 1305 a group of 'poor burgesses', claiming that the rich burgesses 'by sinister collusion among themselves' were stopping them using their trading rights as burgesses, preventing them selling wine, cloth or groceries, or dealing in hides and wool. For the rich burgesses Nicholas de Carliol claimed that the 1216 grant gave exclusive rights to the guild, but he could prove no legal basis for this, and the poor burgesses won their case. It was, however a temporary victory.

Arms of Denton

A crisis occurred in the control of town government during the 1340s, centred on John of Denton. Denton, a wool exporter and war-contractor, was mayor in 1333, 1336–7 and 1340, and alienated many in the town by his profiteering, opportunism and suspected corruption. In 1337 all the jurors on an enquiry into the value of land were his relatives, and they implied that certain plots, which really belonged to the Corporation, were owned by the King, who promptly rented them to Denton, including 'the Mydding Place' on the Sandhill. In particular Denton clashed with the Galloways and Scots. At his re-election in 1341, one group of burgesses elected a rival candidate and seized the town gates, and there was rioting. The King took over and ordered an enquiry.

This gave the lesser burgesses a chance to act, and they suggested a new charter, which was adopted in 1342. This included weekly statements of the town accounts and a formal election system to stop disputes. Between 1308 and 1342 12 companies or 'mysteries' had been created within the burgesses: the merchant companies of the woollen merchants (drapers), corn merchants (boothmen), and silk merchants (mercers), and nine lesser crafts companies including the skinners, butchers, smiths and bakers. The election procedure was intricate: each mystery elected two men, and the 24 elected four. These four co-opted another eight, and this group of 12 then elected another 12, and this final 24 elected the mayor! It was clearly a system highly susceptible to pressure and influence.

In 1343 Galloway and his supporters won, and in 1344 they arrested Denton on a charge of aiding the Scottish army. Denton refused to plead, knowing the jury was rigged, and died in jail. Edward III reacted by taking over the town, and setting up a hunt for Denton's 'murderers'. In the summer of 1345 he restored the town's rights, allowing the election of Robert Shilvington, but insisted on an even 'safer' election procedure. Now the mayor and four bailiffs elected seven men, and the group of 12 elected four. These four proceeded as in the 1342 system, but the new rules even more effectively perpetuated the ruling group. The 1342 system was restored in 1371, but it made no dent in the oligarchic control. In 1400 the town became an independent county with its own sheriff.

Arms of Rhodes

Great merchants like Robert Rhodes, Robert Whelpington, and the Harding dynasty dominated the town in the 15th century. Greatest

Arms of Roger Thornton

of all was Roger Thornton, whom later centuries portrayed as the Dick Whittington of Newcastle. In the words of an old verse:

> 'At the Westgate came Thornton in
> With a hap, and a halfpenny, and a lambskin.'

In reality Thornton came from a landed family, probably in North Yorkshire, but he did rise to be a leading merchant, exporting wool and investing in Durham lead-mines, and mayor of Newcastle 10 times between 1400 and 1425. His reputation lived on because of his benefactions to the town, notably the Maison Dieu, built on the Sandhill in 1412 for 13 poor men and women, and later granted by Thornton's son for town use for wedding receptions. The east end of this building survived as part of the Guildhall until 1823. (Similarly, Rhodes probably provided the fine steeple of St. Nicholas's that we still see.) Roger Thornton lived in Broad Chare by the Quayside, and his will in 1429 showed the extent of his property. He had a main London house called Tannersheld in Cheapside, several estates in Northumberland (especially Netherwitton, where his family survived into the 18th century), and numerous houses and plots all over Newcastle. Thornton was buried in All Hallows, with a huge monument of which the magnificent Flemish brass plate with its engraved figures still survives.

Disputes over the trading rights of burgesses continued. In 1438–9 there was an agreement that all burgesses had the right directly to purchase from ships and strangers for their own use (as agreed in the 1342 charter), but not to re-sell, and in 1477 Henry Redpeth, a tailor, was fined 4s. 4d. (22p) for retailing lint and other goods. After a further dispute the royal Star Chamber in 1516 confirmed the trading monopoly of the merchant companies (which had grouped into a Merchant Adventurers' Guild), and altered the election system so that the four men nominated by the 24 had to be former mayors, aldermen or sheriffs, so further strengthening the ruling group. A number of new companies were formed in the 15th century to represent various town crafts and control apprenticeship and behaviour. So in 1442 a Barber-Surgeons company was incorporated to regulate shaving and primitive medical practices: no foreigner (including Scotsmen) was to be taken as an apprentice, no member or apprentice should shave in the town on a Sunday, nor should they interfere with each other's patients. At the annual procession of all the guilds on Corpus Christi day, this company had to meet at Newgate and after the procession perform the Miracle Play of the 'Baptizing of Christ'.

17. Deserted village at South Middleton on the Wansbeck. The houses and gardens are clearly visible, as is the ridge and furrow.

18. The Newe House, Pilgrim Street, Newcastle, on the site of the Franciscan friary. Later the site for Grainger's town planning.

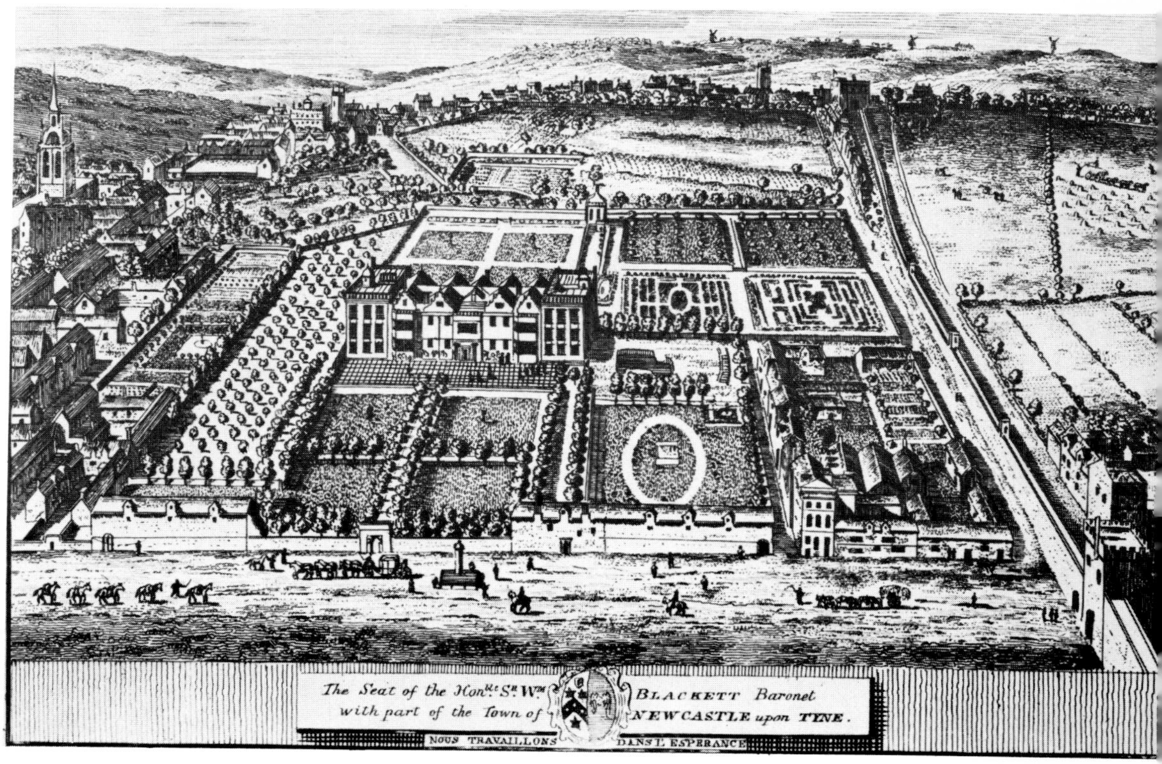

The Seat of the Hon.ble Sr. Wm. BLACKETT Baronet
with part of the Town of NEWCASTLE upon TYNE.
NOUS TRAVAILLONS DANS L'ESPERANCE

19. Upper Coquetdale, looking downriver to Linshiels and Linbriggs. The north bank (photograph left) was part of Kidland, grazed by the sheep of the Newminster monks. The south bank was part of Redesdale Liberty.

XI Tudor and Jacobean Northumberland

The Barbican, Alnwick Castle

The re-establishment of stable government under the Tudors after 1485 did not end the Anglo-Scottish border warfare, which intermittently flared up. After peace from 1497 to 1511 there was the campaign which led to the Scots' disaster at Flodden Field, there were minor invasions in 1522–23, and lengthy conflict in the 1540s. But if the Tudors were unable to halt the border conflicts, they had a more deliberate policy towards the border magnates, notably the Percies. To destroy any potential threat to royal supremacy the Tudors and their servants Cardinal Wolsey and Thomas Cromwell systematically undermined the influence of the Percies as border lords. Wolsey encouraged the growth of a Crown party in Northumberland: gentry who got state pensions for service on the border and who looked to London and not to the Percy organisation for advancement. In the 1520s and 1530s a group of the Forsters, Whartons, Radcliffes and Grays, led by Sir Reynold Carnaby, formed the core of this anti-Percy party. The fifth Earl was excluded from border office, though he made things so difficult that in 1527 the sixth Earl had to be made Warden as no one else could govern. The power of the Percies was, however, gradually weakened. In the 1530s the split between the sixth Earl and his brothers, Thomas and Ingram, led the brothers into the rebellion of the Pilgrimage of Grace and the Earl into dependence on Cromwell. At his death the earldom became extinct and the estates passed to the Crown. Under Edward VI the Crown party got lucrative leases of Percy lands and former monastic property. However, with the accession of Mary the older border lords became more significant: the sixth Earl's nephew regained the earldom and Percy estates and also the Wardenship of the Marches, which had been in the control of the King and the Crown party since 1537.

After Elizabeth's accession the anti-Percy policies were again pursued. Earl Percy was replaced as Warden of the Middle Marches by the leader of the Crown party, 60-year-old Sir John Forster of Adderstone, near Bamburgh, and in the East March by Lord Hunsdon, a southern civil servant. Such men relied on the Crown for their position and authority, and posed no threat to Elizabeth. During the 1560s the Earl became more isolated until in 1569 he joined the Rising of the Northern Earls, which failed and led to his execution in 1572. His loyalist brother was allowed to succeed him, but not allowed to return to the North, and for the next 60 years the Earls were absentee landlords, not feudal lords. It was the end of feudal Northumberland.

These changes were not all the result of government policy. Attitudes were changing of their own accord through contact with other regions and with commercial Tyneside. The Percy Earls did not get the support they had got earlier: in the 1569 Rising only a small number of Northumbrian gentry, including Tristram Fenwick of Brinkburn and Cuthbert Armorer of Belford, followed the Earl. However, the new border regime did not necessarily lead to border peace or better administration. As feudal attitudes decayed, so feudal methods of warfare such as the muster of tenants grew less effective. The new leaders could not turn out the tenantry. The non-pensioned gentry would not help: in 1542 it was reported 'there is continual spoils and robberies, the countrymen looking through the fingers thereat, bidding such as take pensions of the King's highness to go to the remedy thereof'. The 1540s warfare required royal garrisons and even mercenaries from Europe like the horsemen under Captain Andrea at Glanton and the foot soldiers at Charlton under Captain Ventura, whilst the local gentry 'lieth at home, hawking, hunting and going to weddings . . . to the evil example of others in this most chiefest time'.

The Scottish Reformation after 1559 led to the end of the 'Auld Alliance' with France that had so often led Scotland into war with England. Unfortunately, Scotland remained politically unstable and border disturbances continued. Even after the Treaty of Berwick in 1586, James's resentment at Elizabeth's attitude to him led to conditions more like warfare than peace. On the English side the Crown and its officials had largely broken the border reivers and surnames of Tynedale (Chapter XII), but James was still encouraging the raiders of Liddesdale and Teviotdale. In 1587 Forster wrote to Walsingham: 'I am credibly informed that one of the chief men of Liddesdale was with the King [James], who commanded him and his company to take all that could be gotten out of England'. The ageing Sir John Forster was not noticeably successful in dealing with Scottish raids, and a rival faction led by Sir Cuthbert Collingwood of Eslington was constantly trying to get him out of office. Nor were matters helped by the absenteeism of Lord Hunsdon for long periods, and the general reluctance of southern officials to stay in the winter wilds of Northumberland. Incidents were plentiful. At a border meeting at Windy Gyle in 1585 Forster's son-in-law, Lord Francis Russell, was killed. Edmund Craster, a member of the Forster faction, was

Arms of Sir John Forster

also there and helped Forster draft a report to Lord Burghley. In the 1590s Robert Carey, Hunsdon's son, reported that the Northumbrian gentry of the Scots' raiding routes paid blackmail, and in 1587 there had been a major raid of 400 horsemen on Haydon Bridge. In 1596 a band of Sir Robert Kerr's men rode into Alnwick itself, and the following year 30 horsemen attacked Sir John Forster's house 'but that by good happ being espyed coming up the staires his lady gott the chamber doore put to and bolted'.

Ruined pele at Doddington

The end of border conflict came with the Union of the Crowns in 1603, when James VI of Scotland succeeded Elizabeth. James was ambitious for the full unification of the two countries (much of which was not achieved until 1707) and called the English and Scottish border countries his 'Middle Shires'. In 1607 he said 'The Borders of the two Kingdomes are now become the Navell or Umbilick of both Kingdomes'. The Wardenships and the March or Border Laws were abolished, and life became more like that in more southern counties. At Berwick (which had changed hands no less than 13 times since 1296 and where the trading life had been ruined by the wars) the almost total withdrawal of the garrison damaged the local economy, but in general the Union prospered the county. There were still, as elsewhere, factional disputes amongst the gentry, but 'by 1611 the overwhelming majority of the inhabitants of Northumberland were as law-abiding and deferential towards those in authority as people in any other part of England' (S. J. Watts), though that year saw the last of the border raids. Robert Elliot of the Redheugh in Liddesdale rode with 50 horsemen to Lionel Robson's house at Leaplish in North Tynedale, killed Robson and others and broke down his house with their axes.

Nowhere can the decline of feudal attitudes in Northumberland be seen better than in the changes in farming and land management during the Elizabethan and Jacobean years. Landlords began to view their land in a more commercial, profit-making light, rather than as capable of supporting so many men for the declining border musters. The Percies themselves were pioneers in this. The Earl's agent, George Clarkson, had surveyed the estates in 1567, and in the early 17th century the absentee Earl had land-surveyors draw up detailed maps of his villages and fields, such as that for Acklington in 1616 (Plate 16). Suggested improvements included rationalising the allocation of strips in the village fields and grouping the demesne lands into one block. This took place at Chatton, Rock and elsewhere, but securing agreement on an equitable distribution was a slow business. The Earl's agents had more room for manoeuvre with his parklands. In the 1560s the parks around Alnwick were still very much

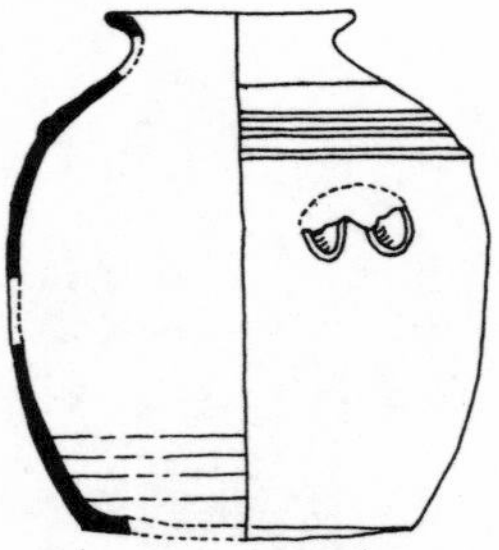

13th-century flagon from West Whelpington

hunting forests, but during the following 50 years they were enclosed for big sheep and cattle farms, and in 1612 Cawledge, Hulne and West Park were all large leasehold farms giving good rents. Crown leases and sales of former monastic lands also provided scope for the commercial farmer, and after the Union of 1603 a series of court cases helped destroy the traditional tenant-right and border tenures that gave inheritable tenancies and low rents in parts of Northumberland, and landlords were able to impose leasehold agreements at rising economic rents.

The declining need to maintain tenants for border service meant landowners could alter the land-use to profitable sheep farming, evicting the villagers and creating new single farms. At Outchester, at the head of Budle Bay, near Bamburgh, sometime before 1580 Thomas Jackson of Berwick expelled the 12 tenants and turned the fields to pasture. The deserted villages (not all of them dating from this period) can often still be seen today, with their streets, house foundations and ridge-and-furrow open-fields fossilised under the grass, as at Halton, Ogle, and South Middleton (Plate 17). The deserted village of West Whelpington, near Kirkwhelpington, has been excavated by M. G. Jarrett, and although not deserted until the early 18th century, has revealed many details of peasant village life. The medieval stone-walled houses grouped around a green were primitive, most having only one room; even the rebuilt 17th-century village had similar houses with open-hearthed fires, though they acquired glazed windows and some had locks.

The change to sheep farming did not always mean mass evictions and depopulation. Many villages were already 'decayed' by the Scottish wars, plague and migration, and these villages were the most susceptible to conversion. William Selby, Northumberland M.P., and son of the Newcastle hostman, defended the enclosures in Parliament, arguing that the county 'was so nigh Scotland, and their countrey was so infected with the Plague, that not only whole Families, but even whole villages, have been swept away with that calamity'. In many cases the new farms must have absorbed much of the available local labour. When Sir Robert Delaval bought out the 15 tenants at Hartley in south-east Northumberland in the 1570s and converted to grass, six tenants got new holdings in Seaton Delaval and five others cottages in Hartley, though Sir Robert later also converted Seaton Delaval. But by 1600 the main wave of conversions was over as prices shifted, and in the following years Delaval was converting back to mixed husbandry. Despite all these changes, however, Northumbrian agriculture, especially outside the coastal plain, was still in 1625 very backward compared with southern England.

XII The Border Dales

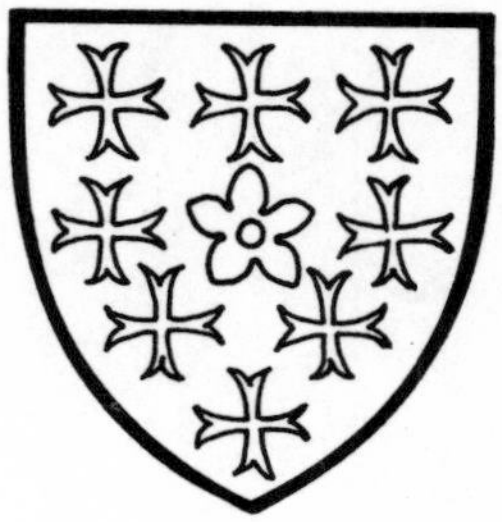

Umfraville Arms

In the late medieval period the Northumbrian valleys of Redesdale and North Tynedale developed a wild society very distinct from the rest of Northumberland. To some extent this distinctiveness may go back to the sparse Anglian settlement of these valleys, as the many Celtic place-names testify, and to the strongly pastoral economy. In the main, though, it was the result of the medieval history of the area, combined with the physical isolation of these narrow border dales, cut off from the rest of the county by wide moorlands.

In Norman times, North and South Tynedale became a Liberty, long held by the Scottish king, whilst Redesdale was granted as a Liberty to the Umfraville family, barons of Prudhoe. The Redesdale Liberty included not only the Rede valley itself, but all the south bank of the Coquet upstream from Holystone, so that one finds places in upper Coquetdale described as in Redesdale. The Umfraville headquarters in Redesdale were at Elsdon, until, by command of Henry II after 1157, they built the castle at Harbottle.

Although Redesdale and Tynedale were outside royal jurisdiction for long periods, there is no sign of greater lawlessness than elsewhere in Northumberland. In the 1160s, during a period of royal control, Henry II's judges were chasing Richard of Emmethaugh, up in Kielder, for the last 10s. (50p) of a fine, whilst the Assizes of the Scots' king, as lord of Tynedale, held at Wark-on-Tyne in 1279, and Edward I's Assize in 1293 portray much the same picture as the 1256 Northumberland Assizes. There are detailed enquiries about minor thefts, and coroners' reports on tragic deaths, such as the child who perished 'in quodam cacabo pleno aqua calida', 'in a pot full of boiling water', or the several people who died of cold on the moors between Bellingham and Haltwhistle. It is a sad picture, but not one of a lawless society. As elsewhere in Northumberland, 1150 to 1300 saw economic expansion in the border dales, with settlement and shielings spreading. By 1300 there was extensive arable land at Ridlees and Quickening Cote on the southern flanks of upper Coquetdale. Routes led through the hills into Scotland, with meeting points on the border line where international disputes could be settled. Gamelspath, the upper stretch of Dere Street to the border, is noted as such a point in the 1249 'Laws of Marches'.

Badge of Bishop Fox

The Scottish wars destroyed this way of life. The dales were prime targets for Scots' raiding groups, burning crops and stealing cattle. Remote upland shielings and farms were soon abandoned. The border dales also suffered because as Liberties they were particularly susceptible to breakdowns in lordship and law enforcement. After Edward I's seizure of Tynedale in 1290, North Tynedale was re-granted six times in 40 years, largely to absentees, finally being sold to Queen Philippa in 1336. Clearly order broke down, for after Philippa's death the people of Tynedale petitioned the King in 1369–73 for the restoration of law and administration in the valley. In Redesdale the gradual retreat of the Umfravilles to their Lincolnshire lands had a similar effect. In the absence of effective rule, extended kinship groups or 'surnames' sprang up to supply a type of law and order. As Dr. J. A. Tuck has noted, social anthropologists have found such reactions in many societies when lordship collapses. In North Tynedale the Charltons were the main surname, together with the Dodds, Robsons and Milburns, and in Redesdale it was the Halls together with the Reeds, Hedleys, Dunns, Potts and Fletchers. On the Scottish side the lowland clans or surnames of the Armstrongs, Croziers, Elliotts, Nixons and others also sprang up in the 14th and 15th centuries.

Blood-feuds, alliances and thieving between the surnames often ignored the Border itself. It was a wild, cruel society. In 1498 Bishop Fox of Durham issued his 'Monitio contra famosos latrones de Tynedale', admonition against the notorious thieves of Tynedale, excommunicating many of the inhabitants. Yet this wild society, on both sides of the border, has left us with the melancholy yet moving poetry of the Border Ballads. Perhaps the finest come from the Scots side, but many good ballads originate in the English valleys, such as *The Death of Parcy Reed.* This records the death of Percy Reed of Troughend and Keeper of Redesdale, who got into feud with the Croziers. Reed was lured into a Crozier ambush on Carter Fell by his neighbours, the Halls, whilst out hunting with them.

The Tudor kings and their servants did not look kindly on these surnames. The special status of North Tynedale was formally abolished by Henry VII, and that of Redesdale in 1546, but so long as the Marches were left under control of the border magnates like the Percies and Dacres, the surname tribes were not suppressed. The patronage of the border lords perpetuated the surnames, whom the Percies found useful for border raids or personal quarrels. Playing with these groups was a dangerous game, however. In 1523 the Earl of Northumberland used them in a Scottish raid and wrote to Henry VIII promising 'to lette slippe secretlie them of Tindaill and

Riddisdaill for th'annoyance of Scotland—God sende them all goode spede', with Sir Ralph Fenwick to lead the Tynedale men and Sir William Heron the Redesdale men. But only 10 months later when Sir Ralph went into Tynedale with 80 horsemen to arrest the outlaw William Ridley for murder, William Charlton of Bellingham got together 200 men and 'set upon the said Sir Rauff . . . (and) chased the said Sir Rauff out of Tyndaill'. Retribution from the royal officers was swift, but this sort of incident was common. The surnames were also ready to ally with the Scots. In March 1524 William Franklin wrote from Durham to Cardinal Wolsey that 'the Hyland theeves with banyshed men, to the numbre of foure hundread men, accompanyed with many Scotts, came to Ingoo and Kirkheton, in Northumberland, and overrane the countrey too within eight myles of Newcastell, when they slew seven mene out of hande, and hurte dyvers moo in perell of dethe, setting fyer on the said townes, and drove away all the goodes and cattaill lying in their way'. It is scarcely surprising that the Merchant Adventurers of Newcastle agreed in 1554 that they should not take any apprentice 'to serve in this Fellysshype of non suche as is or shalbe borne or brought up in Tyndall, Ryddisdall, or anye other suche lyke places' because they were not of 'honest conversation', nor that a line of night watches set up 'at diverse places, passages and fords, endlong all the said Middle Marches, for the better preservation of the same from thieves and spoils' should run *east* of Tynedale and Redesdale.

16th-century Charlton spur

The decline of the surname groups came after 1560, when Elizabeth replaced Earl Percy as Warden of the Middle Marches by Sir John Forster, a lowland Northumbrian squire, and support for the groups ceased. Key jobs were given to outsiders, and offending headsmen were dealt with severely. The ending of surname patronage led the surname leaders to seek acceptance as equals of the lowland gentry, and it is significant that in the 1580s Edward Charlton went to the Court of Requests in London in a dispute with the Halls rather than starting a feud. The 1570s and 1580s were a period of many Scottish raids, when men like Buccleugh tried to revive old feuds, and the decline of the surname groups was not always smooth, but 'by 1601 the Northumbrian surnames were of little significance' (S. J. Watts).

One feature of these Elizabethan years is quite notable. In a series of surveys in 1541, 1550 and 1584 royal commissioners enquired into the decay of border fortifications and organised improvements. In contrast to the castles and peel towers of the rest of Northumberland, they found few stone buildings at all in Redesdale and North Tynedale. Sir Robert Bowes found in 1541 that there even the headsmen had houses 'made of great sware oak trees, strongly bound and joined together with great tenons of the same . . . The timber, as well as the said walls and roofs, be so great, and covered for the most part with turf and earth, so that they will not easily burn or be set on fire'. After 1560, with the decay of surnames and under government encouragement, the distinctive stone bastle-houses were built in these dales, and many of them, with their strong walls and living quarters above the ground-floor animal shelters, can still be seen in the statutory defensive zone set up by the Elizabethan parliament within 20 miles of the border.

With the transition from Border to Middle Shire, these over-populated, poor valleys changed. Many sought occupations outside, notably as Tyneside keelmen. Agriculture improved, and very quickly after 1603 landlords were altering traditional tenures into lease agreements. As early as spring 1604, farmers were re-occupying the upland pastures of Coquetdale, long deserted. In 1608 the Earl of Northumberland was granting 21-year leases at £40 a year on highland cattle pastures and promising permanent 'winter houses where yet never may have been'. But it was in the late 17th and 18th centuries that seasonal grazing gave way to all-year pastoral farming and shielings were replaced by neat Georgian farmsteads. Northumberland provided a refuge for many Scots dissenters persecuted in the Killing Time after 1660, and in the mid-18th century the Rev. Dodgson of Elsdon noted that 'The greater part of the richest farmers are Scotch dissenters'.

The old border routes over Redeswire and Carter Bar became important as drove roads for the southward movement of Scottish cattle to the growing industrial and urban markets in England, and in Northumberland to the great cattle market at Stagshaw Bank, outside Corbridge. Bailey and Culley record that in the early 18th century 'Mr. J. M. Bates, of Aydon White House, bought a Gaellic grammar . . . to converse with the Highland Drovers of Stagshaw Bank who could speak hardly any English'. The routes across the border were also used down to the 19th century for smuggling, for English and Scots excise duties were often different. In 1830 the English tax on a gallon of whisky was 7s. 6d. (37½p), but the Haddington rate only 3s. 4d.(16½p). Whisky was also illegally distilled in the hills, as at Rory's still in Upper Coquetdale, dateable to the early 19th century by Newcastle pottery found in excavations there. Dutch gin and other commodities also found their way from Boulmer, the main smuggling village on the Northumbrian coast, over the border to Scotland. An old Cheviots rhyme says:

Gatehouse bastle

'Jimmy Turner, of Ford, did not think it a sin,
To saddle his horse on a Sunday, and ride to Boulmer for gin.'

XIII Early Coal Mining

15th-century iron forging

The coal trade, on which the North-east was to build its industrial and economic prosperity in later centuries, existed on Tyneside as early as the 13th century. Where the coal seams were near the surface, as to the west of Newcastle, the coal could be won by digging simple bell-pits and, after exhausting the coal at the bottom, digging another further on. As early as 1256 jurors were complaining that the road from Corbridge to Newcastle was dangerous 'per fossas et mineras', especially at night. In 1315 there were mines at Marden (Cullercoats) and Cowpen, and in 1357 the Newcastle burgesses got a royal licence to dig in 'le Castelfield', 'le Frith' (the Forth) and the 'Castelmor' (the Town Moor).

This early coal was mainly used industrially, to burn lime for building, and to smelt iron. In 1291, 80 quarters of coal from Newcastle were sent to Corfe Castle in Dorset for building work, and in the 13th century Nicholas of Acton granted the Cistercian monks at Sturton Grange on Warkworth Moor the right to get coal (or sea-coal as it was long known) from his wood called Midilwode, for their forge. Although there was a Sea-coal Lane in London as early as 1228, coal was not welcomed as an alternative to wood as a domestic fuel. In 1298 men in London refused to work at night 'propter putridenem carbonis marine', because of the stench of sea-coal.

Newcastle built up a thriving trade in coal during the 14th century. The first recorded shipment to London was in 1305, when Thomas Migg took wine from London to Berwick in the *Welfare,* and returned with coals from Newcastle. By 1377 the port was shipping about 15,000 tons a year, but this did not rise substantially for another 150 years. As well as the English coastal trade this included substantial exports to the Continent, mainly for use in smelting, building, smoking fish, and brewing. The main sales were to France, Flanders, and Zeeland, and in 1380–81 there were 118 foreign sailings of coal ships from Newcastle to 39 different ports, the two main ones being Veere in Zeeland, and Kampen in Holland.

In the 16th century there was a dramatic expansion of coal-mining on Tyneside. The increasing shortage of wood in England for fuel and ship-building, especially in Elizabethan times, and a grudging acceptance of coal as a substitute fuel, led to a rapid growth of demand on the London market. In some circles the dislike died slowly: as

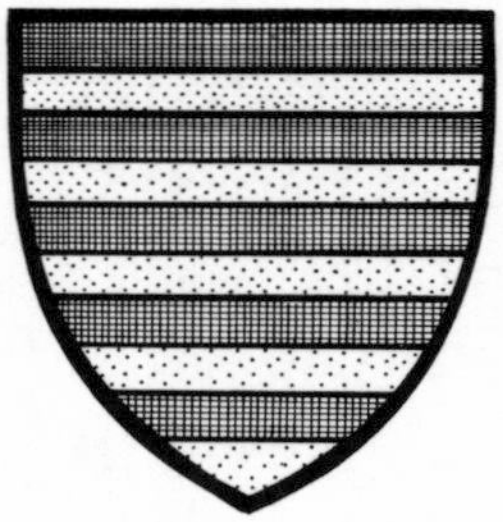

Sir William Selby's Arms

late as 1598 John Stowe recorded that the 'nice dames of London' would not 'come into any house or roome where sea-coales were burnt, or willingly eat of the meat that was either smoked or roasted with sea-coal'. The prohibitive cost of land-transport of coal meant the riverside mines of Tyneside, with sea-transport to London, became the main source. The supply of Tyneside coal also increased through what Professor Trevor-Roper called the 'Capitalist Reformation'. The Church and monasteries had owned many of the coal-bearing lands in Durham and Tyneside, and they had restricted output, but after the Dissolution in the 1530s and increasing royal control of the Church, these lands came into the hands of commercially-minded entrepreneurs, willing to invest capital and take risks for profit. When the Prior of Tynemouth leased out his Elswick mines in 1530, he limited output to 31 tons a day, but when Henry Anderson later leased them from the Crown, there were no such restrictions.

Coal shipments from the Tyne grew rapidly: at the start of Elizabeth's reign they were 32,951 tons in the year, by the end 162,552. By 1608-9 they were 239,261 tons, rising to 452,625 in 1633-4, and 616,000 tons by the end of Charles II's reign. Most went to the London market, but some went to meet a growing foreign demand: in 1552 Thomas Barnabe noted the 'thing that France can lyve no more without than the fysh without water, that is to say, Newcastle coals'. The expression 'salt to Dysert or colles to Newcastell' is found in 1583, and another contemporary referred to Tyneside as 'the Black Indies'.

The bulk of the coal came from 20 to 25 collieries on both sides of the Tyne west of Newcastle. On the north there were pits around Elswick, Benwell, Denton, and Newburn, and around Gateshead and Whickham on the south. Here the coal seams were close to the surface, but an overland haul of three miles could add 60 per cent. to the cost of the coal, and mining had to remain close to the river. The mining expansion was mainly in terms of deeper shafts, most over 15 fathoms deep, and drainage of water from the pits was helped by the new German pumping techniques. The fleets of tall-masted colliers could not sail up the shoally Tyne west of Newcastle, and keels or lighters had to ferry the coal from the staithes to the ships anchored down river as far as North Shields. In 1516 the keelmen were listed amongst the craft guilds of Newcastle, but the guild is not mentioned in later years and the keelmen became an industrial proletariat, largely made up of seasonal workers (since coal was not shipped in the winter months) from Scotland and the Northumbrian dales.

Only Newcastle burgesses or freemen could trade and ship coal on the Tyne, and 'host' or act as middle-men for outside merchants and buyers. As well as controlling the keels these 'Hostmen' (an informal sub-group of the Merchant Adventurers) also gained control of the mining itself. A 99-year lease, known as the Grand Lease, of the richest coal-lands around Gateshead in the Durham Bishopric, was acquired, through a chain of lessees, by Henry Anderson and William Selby of Newcastle on hehalf of an inner ring of these Hostmen and largely purchased with Newcastle town funds. The Hostmen also acquired leases north of the river and refused to deal with non-Hostmen producers, and this gave them a virtual monopoly of the Tyne coal trade. In practice the trade was controlled by a leading group of under 20 Hostmen, known locally as the 'Lords of Coal'. There was opposition to this monopoly, both inside the town and from the London buyers, but in 1600 Elizabeth I granted a charter to the Hostmen, recognising their monopoly in return for a tax of 1s. (5p) on each chaldron of coal shipped, and also granted a new town charter that gave the Hostmen effective control, though in town government they ruled through their membership of the Merchant Adventurers' Company. The same man, William Jenison, became both mayor and first Governor of the Hostmen, William Jackson became town clerk and company clerk, and the 10 aldermen were all original members of the Hostmen's company, nine of them Grand Lessees. Of the 28 mayors of Newcastle between 1600 and 1640, only William Warmouth, a merchant, was not a Hostman.

Seal of Hostmen

Landowners on Tyneside who tried to by-pass the Hostmen's monopoly and run their own coal production and marketing were unsuccessful: the Earl of Northumberland tried it with his mines at Newburn, but was soon leasing them again to Hostmen. Nor was it simply industrial muscle on the Hostmen's part. As pits became deeper, sinking new shafts required more capital, capital that would be lost if the seams were missed (only in about 1615 were boring rods introduced, and experts were few). Coal was only shipped in the summer months, and final payment on the London market might only come a year after the coal was first dug. Building staithes and winter storage was expensive. As Gray said in his *Chorographia* in 1649, colliery ownership was 'a great charge, the profit uncertain'. The cartel of the Hostmen had economies of scale on its side, the lone entrepreneur had to take the high risks himself. The only non-Hostman to make a steady income out of coal was Anthony Errington of Denton, who built up enough fortune between 1602 and 1622 to construct his fine hall at Denton.

Outside the main Tyneside mining area there were other small, accessible seams. Coal for very local use was mined near Berwick, Shilbottle, Acomb (Hexham), and along the Northumbrian coast.

In Elizabethan Tynemouth there were small mines in the town-fields, pits five fathoms deep, which took 12 days to sink and cost £2 each, but which produced 38 tons a day. There were also pits at Whitley and Hartley. At Amble in 1590 a rent of £2 was paid for 'all mynes of coales ther and in Auxley' (Hauxley), and at Bilton the 1624 map shows two rows of pits. There were collieries at Cowpen and Bedlington, but the ventures were short-lived and the mines frequently abandoned. In 1605 Huntingdon Beaumont, a southern mining adventurer, and Peter Delaval, a London merchant member of the Delaval family, invested some £6,000, a huge sum, but the mines were abandoned in 1614. They had built the first wagonway, a track on which horses could pull the coal-wagons, from Bebside to Blyth for shipment, and later Delaval came back and carried off 'all the said rayles set upon the land and ground of Bebside for 500 paces in the wagonway'. As Gray commented of Beaumont: 'within few yeares he consumed all his money, and rode home upon his light horse'. These coastal shipments from Amble, Blyth and Cullercoats amounted in the early 17th century to some 2,000 tons, but this was only about one per cent. of the Tyne trade.

The growth of the coal-trade stimulated some ancillary industries, which used the small coal not worth shipping, coal from the outlying coastal pits, and coal produced by non-Hostmen. The oldest was salt production by the evaporation of sea-water. In 1408 William de Whitchester held 'a salt-cote' in Seaton Delaval and in 1564 the traveller, Dr. William Bullein, noted Sir John Delaval's pans at Seaton Sluice. The salt from these pans was sent from Blyth to Yarmouth for curing herrings. In the 16th and 17th centuries very substantial numbers of saltpans were set up at both North and South Shields. The other, much newer industry was glass-making, for which the use of wood as fuel was banned in 1615. By 1619 Sir Robert Mansell had established a factory by the mouth of the Ouseburn at Byker, run by French Huguenots from Lorraine. By 1740 he had three furnaces and employed 60 people. The plant produced 3,000 cases of glass each year, and the Tyne was the principal source in the country of window glass.

Tyne keel

XIV The Civil War

The late 1630s saw a growing conflict between Charles I and land-owning and business interests over his autocratic government, imposition of taxes like ship-money, and promotion of High Church practices. The first spark in the north was when the Scottish Presbyterian army, in revolt against Charles' imposition of a Prayer Book on the Scottish Church, crossed the border in 1639, and again in 1640 when they occupied Newcastle and the Tyneside coalfield after routing the King's forces at Newburn on the Tyne. They forced the King to recall Parliament, and withdrew in 1641, but during their stay Newcastle had to pay them £200 a day.

As civil war grew nearer the bulk of the county gentry of Northumberland (with some notable exceptions like the Ogles of Eglingham) supported the King, but the merchants of Newcastle were more divided. Local conflicts, particularly that between the inner ring of governing Hostmen like Sir John Marley, Sir Thomas Riddell and Sir Nicholas Cole, and those slightly outside this group, still dominated town politics. There was a small but significant Puritan community, established in the town since the days of John Knox's residence and helped by trading links with Scotland and Protestant Northern Europe. Dr. Robert Jenison, son of a former mayor, was a leading Puritan clergyman and several merchants like Sir Lionel Maddison, Henry Dawson and Robert Bewick were Puritans. As a group they were not clearly associated with either the inner or outer ring, but included members of both. However, a group of High Churchmen led by Marley were enthusiastic in the attempts of Secretary Windebanke to suppress Puritan activity, and in 1640 Jenison had to flee to Danzig in North Germany. Later that same year, as Mayor Bewick welcomed the Scots, men like Marley and Cole fled to Kings Lynn. The Scottish occupation made the Puritan group unpopular in the town and Cole was elected mayor. Nevertheless, the Newcastle M.P.s in the Long Parliament were not clearly aligned: both Anderson and Blakiston voted against the King's minister, Strafford, though Anderson later became a Royalist, and the Puritan Blakiston a Parliamentarian and regicide.

Arms of Sir John Marley

Charles saw the strategic importance of controlling the Tyne: coal exports could buy foreign armaments, and the river provided an entry port for both arms and men. In June 1642 he sent the Earl of Newcastle as governor, and Sir John Marley was appointed Mayor. The presence of royal troops secured Newcastle as a royalist town. There was still opposition: at Tynemouth Castle labourers in the coal trade resisted the Earl's troops, and in Newcastle Marley had to purge the Corporation: Warmouth, a leading Puritan alderman, was dismissed in April 1643, and in September Marley disfranchised 35 freemen, including the Dawsons.

This royalist control worried the Parliamentarians. On 14 January 1643 Parliament put an embargo on trade with the Tyne 'Vntill that Towne of Newcastle shall be freed of, and from the Forces there now raised, or mainteined against the Parliament'. The embargo on coal was easily enforced since most of the colliers were based in the Thames or East Anglia, though the stoppage caused hardship in London. Other ships still got into the Tyne, however. In May 1643 Parliament sent the *Antilope* on a cruise up the north-east coast, where it reported from Holy Island roadstead that it had captured off Tynemouth bar two Kings Lynn ships that had just delivered corn to Newcastle. In January 1644 a Danish boat brought guns from Amsterdam to Newcastle.

Parliament was in no position to take military action against Newcastle, deep in the royalist north, but in September 1643 the Solemn League and Covenant with Scotland brought in Scottish troops on the Parliamentary side. The following January these troops under Lord Leven advanced into Northumberland in a winter so severe that many crossed the Tweed over the ice. Sir Thomas Glemham, commanding royalist troops in the county, realised he could not resist this force, and withdrew from Alnwick to Newcastle, destroying the bridge over the Aln first. The Scots took Alnwick, Coquet Island (which had a royalist garrison) and on 28 January captured Morpeth (where William Craster was royalist governor for part of the Civil War). As Leven advanced on Newcastle, the Marquess of Newcastle managed to slip into the town with reinforcements. There were skirmishes around the town, notably at Shieldfield fort, and Marley destroyed the suburbs around Newgate and Sandgate, the fires 'burning all that night, and Sunday and Monday all day', so that the Scots could not get near the town walls. Leven decided to press on south rather than undertake a siege, and moved into Durham, where he captured South Shields, which gave him command of the Tyne entrance, and then advanced into Yorkshire.

Newgate

The royalists recaptured Morpeth, and Parliament asked the Scots to send more troops to help take Newcastle. These arrived in June, followed by Leven's troops in August after the victories at Marston Moor and York. Newcastle was surrounded, with bridges of boats stretched across the Tyne at Elswick and Ouseburn, and the siege began. The delay since February had, however, given Marley time to improve the town's defences. The ditch outside the walls was deepened and the outer sides of the walls were 'steeply lyned with clay-mixt earth' to stop besiegers climbing up. Gaps in the battlements were filled with 'lime and stone', leaving only narrow slits, and stones were collected to drop on attackers. Now the Scots gun batteries began to bombard the town, and troops mined under the walls. In particular, the fire of the Gateshead guns forced many inhabitants to flee from the lower parts of Newcastle to the upper town beyond St. Nicholas's. The guns on the Leazes breached the wall around St. Andrew's, but this, like other holes, was blocked up with timber and rubbish by the townsmen. After Marley several times refused to surrender, Leven attempted a general assault on 19 October. Mines breached the walls at Sandgate and in 55-yard stretches at Westgate and White Friars Tower, as did the artillery, though less effectively. Douglas wrote: 'The mines were easy to enter, but the breaches were weel guarded, and hard to enter; they entered by the help of the mines, for they that entered the mines helped them that were at the breeches to come in: after two hours hard disput the town is taken'. Marley and the leading royalists retreated to the Castle, but were forced to surrender on 22 October. Tynemouth Castle's surrender on 27 October completed the Scots' victory.

Cartoon figures from Gardner pamphlet

The Parliamentary-Puritan group now took over the town's government, especially after the Scots finally left in 1647, and Dr. Jenison became vicar. In general, and particularly during the dominance of the Dawson circle during the 1650s, the outer ring of Newcastle merchants now controlled the town, but the new oligarchy were just as zealous over the town's monopolistic privileges as the old inner ring, and they vigorously opposed the attempts of Ralph Gardner of Chirton to establish at North Shields in the 1650s trading rights free of Newcastle. At the Restoration the Puritans were driven out of power, but many of the leading Newcastle merchants, like Shafto and Blackett, were no more committed Puritans than committed royalists, and those with the right trading and family connections retained their positions after 1660: Mark Milbank, for example, was sheriff in 1638 (though not one of the inner ring of Hostmen), mayor in 1658, a Hostman in 1662, and mayor again in 1672. During the Commonwealth, Puritanism took a greater and lasting hold on the religious life of the town, and in the Northumbrian countryside with ministers like John Lomax at Wooler, and Ralph Ward at Hartburn. Although most of the Puritan preachers were ejected in 1660 (Lomax went to North Shields where he found a

Wall Knoll tower

living as a physician and ran an apothecary's shop), many of the congregations survived, augmented by the efforts of the Scottish dissenting ministers like William Veitch, who fled from the religious persecution of the 'Killing Time' in Scotland in the 1660s.

After the Civil War royalists on Tyneside and in Northumberland had their estates sequestered, like the Collingwoods of Eslington, or only retained them by paying a heavy fine, like the Claverings of Callaly. In 1648 the royalist rising led by Sir Marmaduke Langdale, who seized Berwick, found some support amongst the Northumbrian gentry, and there were some skirmishes around Alnwick, but it was easily suppressed. The governor of Tynemouth Castle, Henry Lilburne, declared for the King, but the Castle was quickly stormed and taken. In 1655 there was a widespread royalist revolt, but in Northumberland only about 70 men were involved. They met near Newcastle, but dispersed and were easily captured. At this time a greater threat to law and order came from the mounted bands of robbers and horse-thieves, known as moss-troopers, many of them disbanded soldiers, who rode the Northumbrian moorlands.

The war severely damaged the Tyneside economy. The coal trade was at a standstill and most of the mines belonged to deprived royalists. By the early 1650s, however, the coal shipments had recovered. Shortages, stoppages and the dangers from Dutch privateers often helped the Newcastle merchants to get higher prices and profits on the London market, though they reduced the earnings of the keelmen and colliers. A London pamphlet of 1653 *The Two Grand Ingrossers of Coles* accused some Newcastle merchants of using false weather reports and tales of shipwrecks to improve their London prices. Engrossing or getting a corner in a commodity and inflating its price was common practice at this time. William Blackett, who became a prominent merchant in this period, trading to Eastland and dealing in whaling and fishing to Greenland, is reputed to have made a lot of his fortune by taking advantage of a rumour that a fleet from Eastland had been sunk to make a quick profit on his own goods at inflated prices. Although coal shipments and overseas trade soon recovered, other industries found things more difficult. Several of the Tyneside glasshouses had been damaged by the Scots, and the Tyne never regained its virtual monopoly. Similarly, the salt trade was hard hit by the new free competition from Scotland. In contrast, there was a rapid growth in shipbuilding on the river, stimulated by government contracts. In 1651 there were 25 flat-boats under construction for the government.

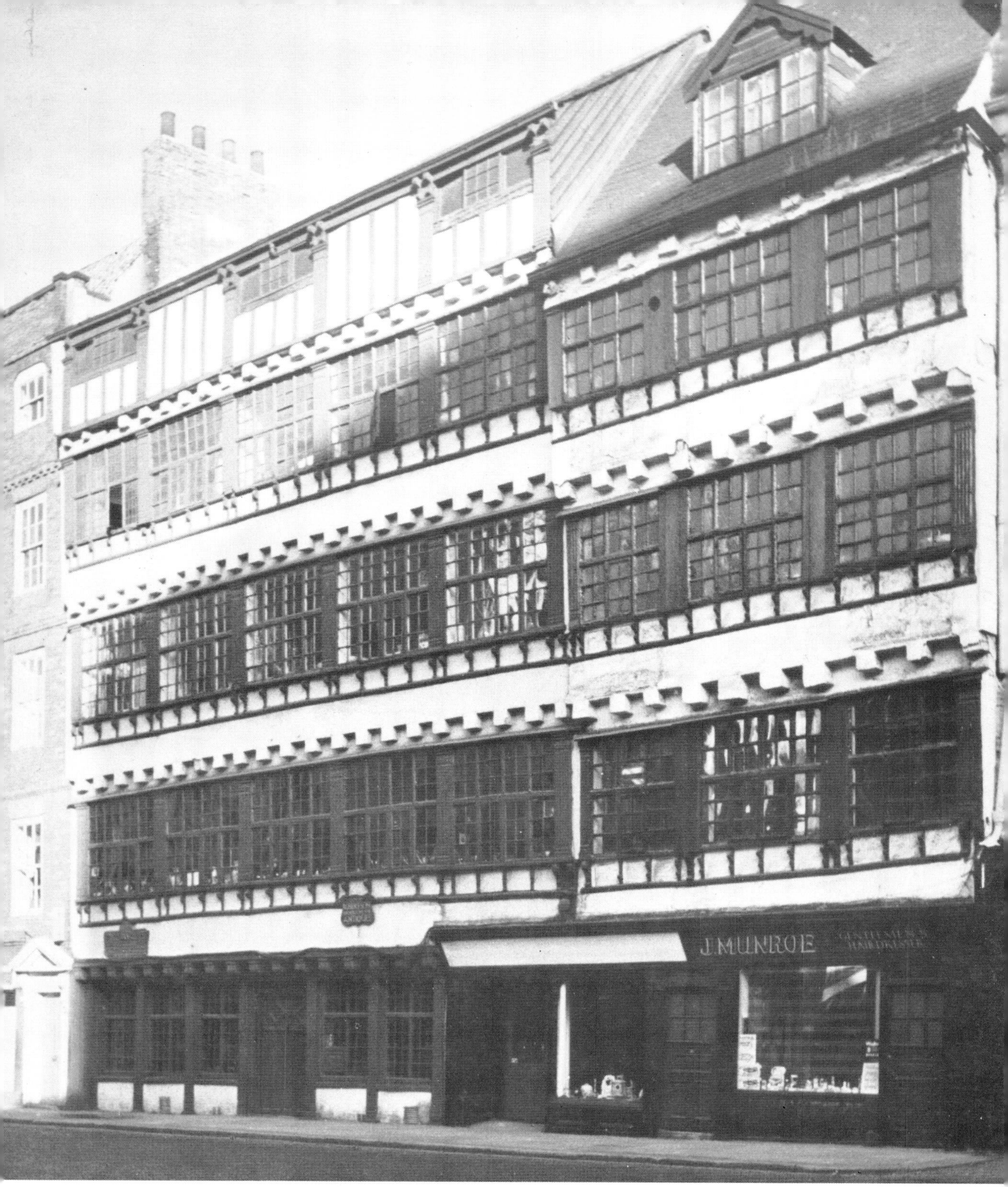

20. 17th century merchants' houses on the Sandhill, Newcastle.

21. Waterfalls Hill, gathering place for the 1715 Jacobite Rising, later marked by a Roman milestone from Dere Street.

22. Dunstan Hall near Embleton, a manor house dating from at least Edward I's reign.

XV Restoration Newcastle

Newcastle in Charles II's reign had changed in several ways since the late middle ages. It still bore many of the features of a medieval town, such as its walls with the gates locked at night, but the religious houses that had occupied so much of the upper medieval town were no longer there. After the Dissolution of the Monasteries these had been mostly sold by the Crown. Black Friars had been leased to nine of the guilds, some of which built halls onto the friary, and parts of the building can still be seen today. Grey Friars and St. Bartholomew's nunnery came into the hands of the wealthy Newcastle merchant, Robert Anderson, who build 'a princely house' and gardens. This house (Plate 18), known as Newe House and later Anderson Place, was situated at the top of Pilgrim Street, described in 1649 as 'the longest and fairest street in the Town'.

Arthur's Cooperage, the Close

Newcastle was a leading provincial city, or in Gray's words, 'the Eye of the North, the Harth that warmeth the South parts of this Kingdome with fire; An Aegypt to all the Shires in the North . . . for bread'. In 1635 Sir William Brereton simply thought it 'beyond all compare the fairest and richest towne in England', though he added that the streets were 'so steep as horses cannot stand upon the pavements–therefore the daintiest flagged channels are in every street that I have seen: hereupon may horses go without sliding'. In 1547 the population was about 10,000. By 1665 it was about 13,400, despite a series of severe plague outbreaks in the century between. The 1635-36 outbreak took over 5,000 lives in Newcastle, and fear of plagues and 'sweating sicknesses' was great. When Ambrose Barnes was a merchant's apprentice and news was brought that a servant was sick, his master is reputed to have got up from dinner, rushed to North Shields and sailed off to Hamburg the same day, leaving Barnes to run affairs.

The commercial and mercantile centre of the town had now definitely moved down on to the Sandhill and Quayside, though the road north of St. Nicholas's was still the main internal market-place. On the Sandhill the medieval Guildhall or Exchange, damaged by fire in 1639, had been largely rebuilt in 1655-58 by Robert Trollope. The original contract was for £2,000, but Trollope eventually charged £9,774, which an embarrassed Corporation had to finance by public loans. Around the Sandhill and in the Close next to it the rich

Arms of Cole

merchants like Sir John Marley, William Blackett, and Mark Milbank had their 'stately houses'. The surviving glass-fronted houses on the Sandhill probably date from this Restoration period (Plate 20). The leading merchants were extremely wealthy: in 1644 Marley was said to be worth £4,500 a year, whilst Sir Nicholas Cole was described as 'fat and rich, vested in a Sack of Sattin'. The inequalities of wealth in Restoration Newcastle can be seen from the Hearth Tax on households with three or more hearths, collected in 1665. Forty-one per cent. of households in the town were exempt, but this overall figure hides local variations. The richest ward, Pink Tower, which included the Sandhill and east end of the Close, had no exemptions, and over one-fifth had more than six hearths. Although the eight central wards of Newcastle had only 18 per cent. of the households, five out of the six aldermen that can be identified lived in these wards around the Side, Sandhill and St. Nicholas's. The figures also reveal the social stratification within the merchant community: the Hostmen who can be identified had an average of 5.7 hearths, whereas the non-Hostmen merchant adventurers averaged 4.3. But the mayors and governors of the Hostmen averaged 8.4, and Marley, Shafto and Milbank had over ten.

The Quayside, running right along to the Sandgate, was a bustling place with 'two cranes for heavy commodities, very convenient for carrying of corn, wine, deals etc.' to and from the ships from Amsterdam, Hamburg and the Baltic. The houses on the Quayside itself were well-to-do, but behind them in Pandon and below All Saints' were the dense households of the poorer classes. The densest and poorest area was the suburb of Sandgate, just outside the east wall of Newcastle by the river. Gray wrote: 'without this gate [are] many houses, and populous, all along the waterside; where shipwrights, seamen and keelmen most live'. Most of the Sandgate houses had only one hearth and 79 per cent. of households were exempted from the Hearth Tax, but there was a lot of suspicion of the collectors, who had to enter houses. It was a period of trade recession and high unemployment, and the collectors were cursed and stoned. The tumult was only controlled when the Mayor, William Blackett, ordered that the tax only be collected from those willing to pay.

Arms of Milbank

The Restoration had returned the government of Newcastle to the royalist group of Hostmen led by Sir John Marley. Non-committed merchants like Blackett and Milbank were able to continue, but Puritans fell under a cloud. Ambrose Barnes, a leading Puritan merchant who had become an alderman in 1658, fell from favour in 1660, and he even contemplated migrating to the Dutch colony of Surinam, where he had business investments. Under the Clarendon

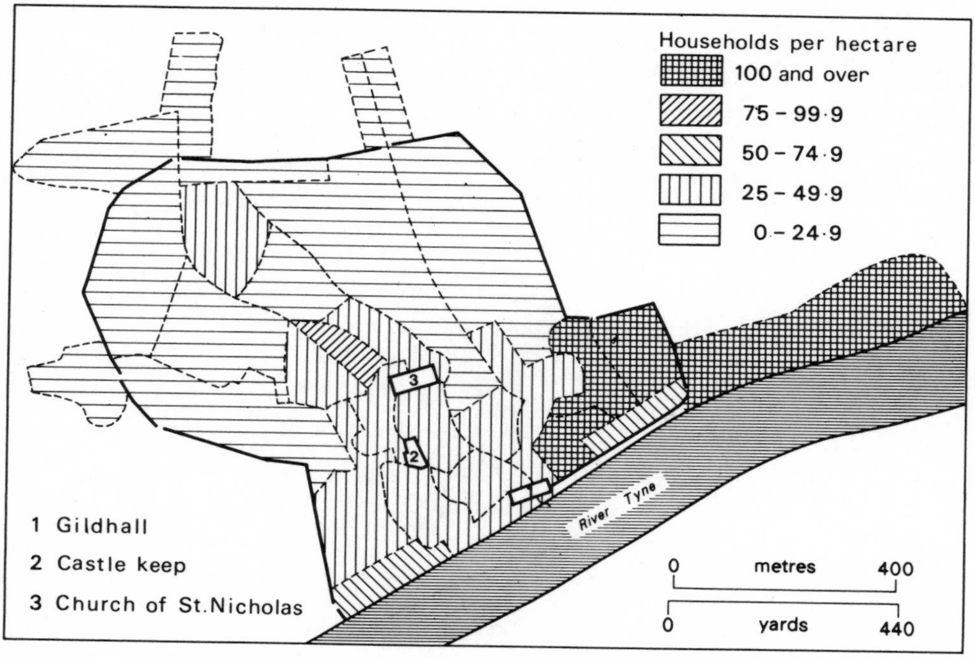

8. Household Density in Newcastle, 1665

Code not only were Puritans and dissenters excluded from town office, but their religious meetings were illegal. The town serjeants spied on the dissenters' meetings held near the White Friars Tower under Richard Gilpin, and in a raid in August 1669 found a congregation of fifty to sixty. Barnes several times found his house in the Close, near to the river, useful for getting across to Gateshead in a boat, while writs were served in Newcastle.

With the accession of James II in 1685 a new toleration seemed to appear. James ordered a new common council of broader religious persuasion. Barnes again became an alderman, and his *Memoirs* comment: 'Men were at a loss to see how suddenly the world was changed, the cap, the mace, and the sword, one day carried to the church, another day to the mass-house, another day to the dissenting-meeting-house'. The toleration was, however, only a step towards the promotion of Roman Catholics in town government. In his last year Charles II had imposed a new charter on the town that gave royal control, but he died before it could take effect. Now James tried a similar policy. In December 1687 he rejected the elected Corporation and demanded named Catholics be elected. Sir William Creagh was appointed mayor, and he agreed to surrender the old charter. At the guild in 1688 the electors refused to accept this and elected William Hutchinson, a leading dissenter, as mayor. In November the town welcomed the accession of William of Orange as King, and James II's flight. Down on the Sandhill a new statue of James II on horseback was pulled down in May 1689, and seven years later 'the Metal y^{t} was left of the Horse part' was used for a set of bells for All Saints' church.

James II statue, the Sandhill

XVI The Jacobite Diversion

Arms of Sir John Fenwick

The overthrow of James II was welcomed in Newcastle because of his interference in town government. However, in rural Northumberland many of the gentry were Catholics and many were supporters of the Stuart cause. In the last months of James II's reign, the Duke of Newcastle had begun to recruit a regiment from amongst the Northumberland gentry to support James. One of his officers was Daniel Craster of Rock. In the early years of the new monarchy the government was concerned lest Jacobite groups in the North-east aid a French assault on the coal trade. In 1691 two French commanders, Claude de Forbin and Jean Bart, landed with eight ships at Druridge Bay and pillaged and set fire to the village and castle at Widdrington, and the orders given to Bart in 1694 to capture 'some fleet of colliers from Newcastle' have survived. In 1696 Sir John Fenwick, M.P. for Northumberland and an ardent Stuart supporter, was arrested for plotting treason. He was convicted by special Act on only one man's testimony (though there is evidence that Fenwick bribed another witness to disappear), and beheaded at Tower Hill on 27 January 1697.

To many Northumbrians Fenwick, 'the flower amang them a'', was a martyr. Events came to a head with the accession of the German George I in 1714. Heavy land taxes to pay for the French war crippled estates that had not yet recovered from the Civil War sequestrations, and many of the Tory gentry saw a Jacobite victory as a way to restore their finances. Lady Cowper wrote later of her relative, William Clavering of Callaly: 'A desperate fortune drove him from home in hope to have repaired it'. Fenwick had sold his Wallington estate to Sir William Blackett of Newcastle to pay off debts. Many estates carried heavy mortgages: in the list of Catholic estates in 1717 after the rebellion Thomas Selby had very extensive lands in upper Coquetdale and around the Cheviots, 'but all the said premises are subject to a forfeited mortgage or other security for £2,000', plus other mortgages to a total of £4,862. The division between the progressive, successful landowners who supported the Whigs and the conservative gentry facing increasing poverty was growing, and Northumberland had many of these Tory backwoodsmen. In *Rob Roy,* Walter Scott draws a portrait of one of these Catholic Tory households in the Osbaldistons of Osbaldiston Hall (believed to be based on Biddlestone Hall, home of the Selbys).

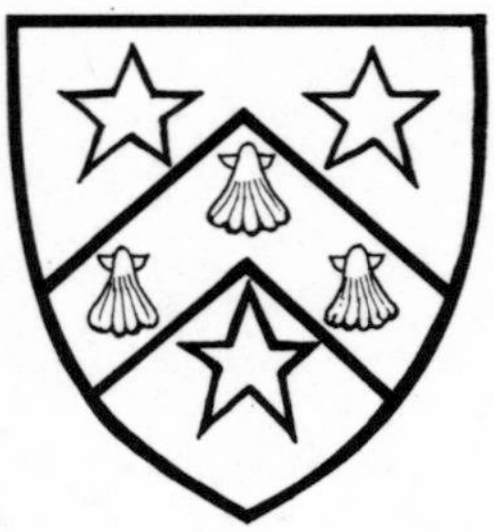

Arms of Blackett

Throughout 1715 there was extensive Jacobite plotting in the region, though this did not worry some government supporters. Sir Henry Liddell wrote to his fellow coal-owner and merchant 'Black William' Cotesworth in January that 'The High party (the pro-Jacobite Tories) are more outrageous than ever which is not unpleasing to me. Did you never see the Gamesters when they dispair'd of success toss about their box and dice?' In September the Highland clans in Scotland declared for James III and the government decided to issue warrants against the leading Northumbrian Jacobites, notably the young Earl of Derwentwater (the Earldom dated from the last year of James II's reign) and the Tory M.P., Thomas Forster of Adderstone. The issue of the warrants provoked these men into open action they might not otherwise have taken. The resolved to 'immediately appear in Arms' so that they would support each other and not be arrested and picked off, one by one.

The support Derwentwater and Forster expected from the Protestant Tory gentry did not materialise. Sir William Blackett, although a symbol of the new commercial gentry, was himself in financial trouble and a Jacobite follower. He was party to the summer plotting and the rebels expected help from him and his many employees in coal-mining and the coal trade. However, when the warrant was issued, he fled south. Lord Derwentwater later complained: 'You see what we have brought ourselves to, by giving credit to our Neighbour tories, as Will Fenwick, Tate, Green and Allgood. If you outlive Misfortune and return to live in the North, I desire you never to be seen to converse with such Rogues in Disguise, that promised to join us, and animated us to rise with them'. If impending bankruptcy was the background to the discontent, it was religion and family links that decided who came out. Nearly all were Catholics, though that included a good proportion of the leading families. There were Lord Widdrington, Clavering of Callaly, George Collingwood of Eslington, Ephraim Selby of Biddlestone, two Swinburne brothers, John Thornton of Netherwitton (descendant of the Newcastle merchant), Lancelot Orde of Weetwood and many more. In *Rob Roy,* 'Sir Hildebrand (Osbaldiston), whose estate was reduced to almost nothing by his own carelessness and the expense and debauchery of his sons and household, was easily persuaded to join that unfortunate standard'. The only leading Protestant was Forster, who brought in his distant relative, Daniel Craster's son, William.

The rebels met at Greenrig near Sweethope Lough on 6 October, but Forster moved them to nearby Waterfalls Hill. Later this spot was marked by the placing on top of the hill of a Roman milestone found on Dere Street close by. It is still there, though now fallen over (Plate 21). Forster brought about 20 men and Derwentwater thirty. Forster was elected leader because of his Protestant religion, though little fitted to the job. They moved north to Plainfield Moor, near Rothbury, and close to many Catholic estates, and more joined them. After a night in Rothbury they rode to Warkworth, where they stayed several days. 'General' Forster, as he now styled himself, proclaimed James III in the market place after Sunday service. They probably stayed in Warkworth as central between moving to occupy Newcastle and moving north to receive supplies from expected French ships. A group under Lancelot Errington did in fact take Holy Island, but the island was quickly retaken by troops from Berwick, and when the French ships arrived a few days later they sailed off north after getting no signal. The delay at Warkworth gave the pro-government party in Tyneside, led by Johnson the Mayor and Cotesworth, time to prepare and get the troops strengthened. The Tyneside keelmen, many of whom were Scots and Jacobite sympathisers, decided to support the government forces.

On 14 October the rebels, now some 300 strong, moved through Felton and Morpeth, and at Hexham learnt of the government hold on Newcastle. After further delay, when they learnt General Carpenter was moving more troops up to Tyneside, they rode north to Rothbury, to meet a southern Scots group under Kenmuir. The joint group then procrastinated along the border under divided leadership, finally moving into Lancashire early in November, expecting great support from the many Catholics and Tories there. The government forces under Carpenter caught them at Preston, where the ill-managed fiasco ended in rebel defeat.

Some prisoners were tried in Lancashire, others taken to London, where they were joined by those from the collapse of the main Scottish rising. Derwentwater was beheaded, but Forster, perhaps with government connivance, escaped from Newgate jail. George Collingwood, unable to travel to London because of gout, was tried and hanged in Liverpool. Many died in jail, such as George Gibson of Stagshaw Close in St. John Lee, who died in Newgate two days after Christmas in 1716. Edward Swinburne also died there, but his brother James escaped. Many did, in fact, escape, and others who survived in jail were freed by an Act of Indemnity in 1717. A number of the lesser rebels, tried at Liverpool, were sentenced to transportation to the American plantations. Cotesworth's schoolboy son, Robert, was visiting Liverpool and wrote home that he had seen the prisoners being taken to the exchange 'to be bound in trades in the plantations' and that they had shouted their continued support for James III. It must have been a cruel transition for these tenants:

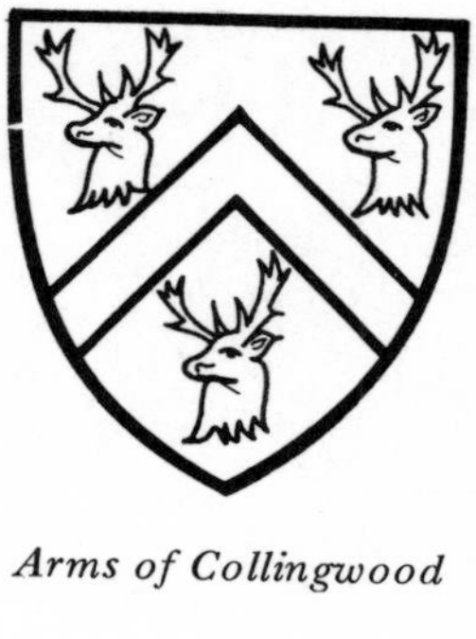

Arms of Collingwood

Arms of Orde

in 12 months from Northumbrian farms by the Coquet or Tyne to the plantations of the Carolinas or West Indies.

Following the '15 there was still a rebellious atmosphere in the county, despite the disaster of Preston. In March 1718 Colonel George Liddell wrote to Cotesworth, then in London: 'Our Torys in this Neighbourhood are grown very insolent and in Northumberland all the Rebels meet as publicly as ever so that I see nothing but the prospect of a New Rebellion'. In April he heard that an 'abundance of transported rebels are actually returned and now in Northumberland: That partys of 40 or 50 well armed are often seen together at Bambrough and several other places where they had Caballs'. But after 1718 the activity and the problem died away, and the rebels were not pursued. Orders were made for the arrest of William Craster at the 1718 Quarter Sessions, but he returned to Rock and died there in 1725.

The aftermath of the 1715 Rising was the forfeiture and sale of many estates, and the replacement of the older gentry by newer groups. The Ordes of Weetwood had to sell up in 1719. They had paid heavily in the rebellion: Lancelot had escaped from jail but lived in exile in Boulogne; his brother, Edward, had been killed; John had been executed; and the fourth brother, Francis, had been jailed until the Act of 1717. The Collingwood's forfeited estate at Eslington was sold to Sir Henry Liddell, the Tyneside coalowner. As Professor Hughes noted: 'Jacobitism was the occasion rather than the cause of the final liquidation of scores of lesser gentry'. The mortgaged estates could stand no more. As Cuthbert Ellison wrote when he had to sell in 1739, 'the mortification was not due to any of my excesses but from an old gangreen'. Some managed to retain their lands, but at high cost. Thomas Thornton bought back his father's forfeited lands at Netherwitton, but the price was £13,250, all raised on mortgages.

Not surprisingly there was little Jacobite enthusiasm in the county during the '45. A few old plotters from the '15, like Bowrie Charlton of Reedsmouth, were arrested by the magistracy. As late as 1780, when the Penal Laws were relaxed, the Misses Charlton walked out of church when prayers were said for King George III, but sentiment had replaced active conviction, and the Duke of Cumberland had been welcomed in the North-east as he pursued the Scots Jacobites in 1746.

XVII Northumbrian Farming and Fisheries

Cheviot Ram

After the turmoil of Civil War and Commonwealth, the later 17th century saw a number of improvements in the farming landscape of Northumberland. In many villages on the coastal plain and in the Tyne valley, the open fields were enclosed by agreement and divided into individual consolidated farms. At Preston, Tynemouth, and Earsdon this was completed as early as 1649. Beadnell was enclosed in 1701, Acomb in the Tyne valley in 1694, and Ovington in 1708. Rennington, near Embleton, was enclosed in 1720, and a 1727 survey said the tenants 'were very poor and scarce able to pay their rents, but since they divided their farmes . . . they have improved their tenements to be worth £25 per annum, and some improved to £30'. Agreement to enclose was often easy to secure because many villages had only a few landowners: when Embleton was enclosed in 1730 there were only six proprietors.

These changes only affected a small part of the landscape. The lowland village fields were simply oases surrounded by much larger unenclosed commons, which completely dominated the upland moors. In the early 18th century the Northumbrian landscape was largely one of open moor and heath, without the hedges, trees and neat fields of today. In the following century this farming scene was transformed by the revolution in agrarian organisation and agricultural techniques. The growing demand from the new industrial regions (like Tyneside itself) led to rising food prices, and good farming profits, especially after 1750. The enclosure of open land allowed better husbandry, and the introduction of sown-grasses, clovers and turnips encouraged new crop-rotations, increased yields, and provided winter feed for the sheep and cattle, so solving one of the major problems of medieval agriculture. As early as 1727 John Proctor of Rock, near Embleton, was growing turnips to feed cattle, and his gardener was in great demand in the locality.

The Stuart enclosures left few open fields to be enclosed by the formal machinery of Parliamentary Enclosure Acts that began to dominate after 1750, but vast moorland areas of Northumberland were enclosed in this way. John Horsley, the Morpeth antiquarian, wrote in about 1729 that 'Great part of the county on the western side is yet waste and almost uninhabited, but much of it has been improved of late years, and the proprietors and inhabitants are yearly improving it still more and more. They have just now this very year divided a large common near Elsdon, and Framlington Moor (part of Rimside) in order to enclose and improve'. Around Wallington, Sir Walter Blackett transformed large tracts of bare landscape with enclosures, farm-buildings and tree and hedge-planting, as did other progressive landowners like the Swinburnes around Swinburne, and the Allgoods around Simonburn. To the south of Hexham the East and West Commons were divided and enclosed in 1752, and many of the individual farmhouses appeared, like that at High Shield built by William Bell. An Act in 1790 enclosed the Shire Moor, near Tynemouth, and amongst other Acts there were 5,000 acres around Tosson in 1805, and the 6,000 acres of Rothbury Forest in 1831.

Farm rents increased earliest on the lowland farms of Bamburghshire and the Tyne valley. Around Corbridge rents doubled from 5s.–7s. (25p–35p) an acre in 1700 to 10s.–15s. (50p–75p) in 1760, and doubled again in 1760–80 with improved farming methods. Although the county continued to have a strong pastoral emphasis, there were many more arable fields than today, even in quite upland areas. Not only was corn grown for home consumption, but an export bounty on corn (in force from 1689 to 1766) encouraged corn exports, and a good deal of corn was shipped from Alnmouth (which began to thrive again as a port), Beadnell and Berwick, to Scotland and to foreign ports. The growing agricultural prosperity and shipments on both sides of the border led to the re-emergence of Berwick in the 18th century as a significant town.

Yields were improved not only by the new rotations, but also by treating the soil, adding marl to light soils and liming heavier soils. Lime had long been used on the Bamburghshire farms; now it became the general practice. Lime-kilns were constructed at Beadnell and North Sunderland, supplying lime to Northumbrian farms, and exporting it to Scotland. At Bent Hall farm near Beadnell the lease in 1800 obliged tenants to spread four double cartloads of shell-lime and eight loads of small lime per acre on fallow land. Turnpike trusts record the carriage of lime across the county, and the small coalfields near Ford were exploited to burn local lime.

Lime kilns, Beadnell

One of the later regions to be improved was Glendale and Tweedside, which had been prosperous in the 13th century, but had suffered greatly in the Scottish wars. On his travels in the 1770s Arthur Young saw large areas here covered in broom and gorse. Agricultural techniques were backward and rents low, but the loamy and sandy soils had a lot of potential and the large areas available attracted enterprising farmers from Scotland and the south, who turned it into the best farming land in the county. The Culley brothers,

Matthew and George, came from Darlington, and beginning at Fenton, near Wooler, in 1767, they worked a number of large farms in Glendale and Tweedside on long leases. They cleared large areas for cultivation, dug drainage ditches, embanked streams and introduced their variant on the famous Norfolk rotation involving a five-six year rotation based on oats, turnips, and barley or wheat, with the other years pasture, so creating the sheep-and-turnip husbandry for which the region became famous.

Fowberry Tower

The Culley's main contribution was in stock-rearing. They bred carefully, creating the Border Leicester sheep as a cross between the Bakewell Dishleys and the Teeswater breed, giving a relatively hardy sheep that fattened rapidly for the Tyneside and West Yorkshire markets. Drill-sown turnips provided winter-fodder. With farmers like the Culleys, John Bailey of Chillingham, and others, the rents rose rapidly, especially during the agricultural price rise of the Napoleonic Wars: farms on the Learmouth estate rose from 5s. (25p) an acre in 1760-80 to 10s. (50p) in 1780-1800, and £1 in 1800-1820. The Culleys' stock was worth £1,297 in 1767, but over £9,000 in 1798, and in 1801 their profit was £4,750. They became landowners, buying Akeld estate and Fowberry Tower, and in 1810 George wrote to his son: 'Whenever I am at Fowberry, I am struck with astonishment, when I reflect on our beginning in Northumberland 43 years ago. To think of my son, now inhabiting *a Palace!* altho' his father in less than 50 years since worked harder than any servant we now have, & even drove a *coal cart*!'.

The change of Northumberland into an efficient farming region is illustrated by the new harvesting technology. Traditionally the grain had to be separated from the straw and chaff by flailing, but in the late 18th century a number of threshing-machines were invented. Northumbrians like Thomas Ilderton of Ilderton and Robert Smart of Hobberlaw pioneered some of the designs, but the first patented working machine was by a Scot, Andrew Meikle, in 1788. The thresher, situated in a wheelhouse, was driven either by horses, water, or wind-power, or later by stationary steam-engines. Many old wheelhouses and chimneys survive on farms, often indicating the former extent of arable farming in areas now mainly pasture. At Harehope, near Eglingham, the four-acre pond constructed to supply water-power to a thresher can still be seen. Northumberland, with its large farms let on long leases, became an early adopter of the machines, and by 1794 Bailey and Culley noted that threshing-machines were 'now becoming common in northern parts of the county', in contrast to the labour-surplus regions of southern England, where there was strong resistance to new machinery. Similarly, when the mechanical reapers of

Thresher wheel-house

McCormick and Hussey (based on an 1812 design by a Northumbrian millwright John Common) were introduced in the 1850s, they were rapidly adopted in the county.

The heavier clay soil areas remained a problem until underfield tile-draining was introduced in the 1840s and 1850s. The Duke of Northumberland was particularly active in this: at Longhoughton 77 per cent. of the acreage was underdrained, at Tynemouth 75 per cent., and Shilbottle 69 per cent., and nearly £1,000,000 was invested on his estates. The improvements were most obvious in south-east Northumberland, but tile-drains were also used to improve loams and 'turnip soils' in Glendale at farms like Learmouth. The downward pressure of rents in the 1840s through fear of Corn Law Repeal meant these investments did not pay off immediately: at East Chevington £1,642 was spent on draining between 1840 and 1851, but net rent to the landlord fell by 29 per cent. Even in the longer term, much of the investment had not paid for itself by the 1880s (the Duke's million yielded only 2½ per cent.), when the era of High Farming gave way to agricultural depression as foreign grain made home production uneconomic. Northumberland, because of its mixed arable and pasture husbandry, did not suffer like the East Midlands, and there were relatively few farming bankruptcies, but the arable acreage contracted, to make Northumberland the dominantly pastoral county it is today. Marginal fields were left to the bracken, and in the coastal plain the arable proportion fell from two-thirds in 1870 to less than one-third by 1929.

There is a long history of fishing on the Northumberland coast. The Lindisfarne monks used to send fish to Durham Priory, and porpoises and seal-calves for special festivals, and in 1225 Prior Germanus of Tynemouth was creating his fishing port at North Shields. Along the coast there were numerous fishing villages, such as Cullercoats, Newbiggin, Alnmouth and Boulmer. The fish caught were mainly for local consumption, though even in medieval times some fish were sent to London. Local salmon caught in the Tweed or off Berwick were renowned, and as late as 1715 Warburton recorded rich salmon catches in the lower Tyne, as many as 265 at one draught. Some local fishermen went further afield: in 1528 six 'craylers' from North Shields were sent to join the Iceland fleet. The fishing villages were also used for smuggling, especially in the 18th century. In 1722 Anthony Mitchell, customs officer at Cullercoats, was murdered by 'two villains that used to run brandy', and in 1762 the customs men seized 400 gallons of rum and geneva, and 2,700 gallons of brandy from Scottish smugglers at Beadnell.

The rise of urban-industrial markets made fishing a focus for commercial investors, and in 1788 John Wood of Beadnell formed the Northumberland Branch of the British Fishery to fish from Beadnell and from Ullapool in Scotland, and built an improved harbour at Beadnell. After this both white fishing and herring fishing expanded along the coast, based especially at Lindisfarne, North Sunderland, Beadnell and North Shields. The herring season in late summer, when the herring came in shoals for spawning, attracted many foreign boats. In 1828 over 100 were using Beadnell, and Scottish girls came to help with the herring curing. At Lindisfarne in the 1860s the harbour might accommodate 100 French boats, and all the local boats' catch was sold for the Stettin market in the Baltic. The coming of the railway made marketing easier, but, together with the increasing size of fishing boats, encouraged concentration on fewer harbours, notably North Shields and North Sunderland. The cobles gave way to larger, decked boats with 40- to 60-foot keels, and in 1877 William Purdy of North Shields converted the Tyne steam-tug *Messenger* into a steam-trawler, and the steam-drifter for herring fishing came in 1907. The number of boats fishing from the smaller harbours like Lindisfarne and Cullercoats declined, and the decline was especially notable at Alnmouth. The inshore herring fishery was over-exploited and the white fish over-trawled, so that by 1914 the fishing fleets were looking further afield, and the coastal fisheries never regained their former importance.

Herring boat of 1890s

XVIII Country Houses and Landed Society

Halton Castle

The tremendous rebuilding of rural England that took place in the south after 1570 is much less evident in the far north. The disturbed state and poverty of the borders meant that very few non-defensive buildings appeared until after the Union of 1603. A late Tudor house, now demolished, was built at Gloster Hill, near Amble, and at Dunstan Hall, near Embleton, there was extensive Elizabethan remodelling of the old house that dates back to the 13th century (Plate 22). After 1603, however, more Northumbrian landowners began adding non-defensive wings onto their peels and castles: at Belsay and Halton in 1614, and more elaborately at Chipchase in 1621.

Very few entirely new houses were constructed until after the Restoration in 1660. At Capheaton the first of Northumberland's real country houses was built for the Swinburnes by Robert Trollope (architect of Newcastle Guildhall) in his eclectic Baroque style. Trollope was an individualist, outside the current architectural idiom of Wren and Inigo Jones, and in Northumberland country houses continued to show mixtures of architectural styles, and often lagged well behind fashions in southern England (as late as 1690 houses with mullioned windows were built at Rock). Trollope also worked at Callaly, and his influence or work can be seen at Bockenfield and Swarland, near Felton. At Netherwitton the Thorntons built their elegant mansion, described by John Horsley as 'stately and magnificent', in 1698 (Plate 23), and at Wallington 10 years before Sir William Blackett had built a new house over the old Fenwick tower.

The main expansion of country house building came later, in the 18th century. This was partly the fruits of agricultural improvement, but also as a result of new industrial and mining wealth. Links between the landed society of Northumberland and the mercantile aristocracy of Tyneside were close, and just as farming profits went into Newcastle banks to fund industry, so successful merchants established themselves in county society, becoming landowners and building country houses. As the Elizabethan Lord Burleigh said, 'gentility is but ancient riches'. Thomas de Carliol, merchant and mayor of Newcastle, had bought an estate at Swarland as early as 1270, and in the 15th century Roger Thornton acquired Netherwitton, where his family still lived in the 18th century. In the late 17th century, the Blacketts established themselves at Wallington, in the 18th the Ridleys at Blagdon, and the

Claytons at Chesters, and in the 19th century the Armstrongs at Cragside. The gentry also found it financially opportune to marry into merchant families: Edmund Craster, who died in 1594, had married Alice, daughter of Christopher Mitford, mayor of Newcastle and governor of the Merchant Adventurers, and Edmund's daughter married into the Andersons of Newcastle. The younger sons of landed families often became apprenticed in the town's leading guilds to seek success for themselves: two of Edmund's sons were apprenticed to merchants, and in the later 17th century William Craster became an Eastland merchant, whilst another Edmund became a barber-surgeon's apprentice in 1713-14.

The major architectural achievement of the first half of the 18th century was also a solitary one: Vanbrugh's magnificent Seaton Delaval Hall, described by the architectural historian, B. Allsopp, as 'classical in idiom and medieval in massing', comparable with the great castles at Dunstanburgh and Warkworth. The main style of Northumbrian country houses in the period 1730 to 1760 was the lighter, classical Palladianism, popularised in the north through the architect James Paine, and which can be seen at Bywell Hall, Belford Hall and Blagdon. At Wallington the Blacketts rebuilt again in Palladian style, replacing the house built only 50 years earlier. Sir Walter Blackett settled some Italian artists at his village of Cambo and they did the interior decorations as well as working at other houses like Callaly and Blagdon. The Northumbrian country houses were built with sandstone or limestone: brick-built houses (like Morwick Hall) or even farms, were only found in the south-east corner of the county.

The design of the gardens around a house was almost as important as the house itself. Seventeenth-century gardens had been formal and geometric, but they were largely destroyed by the landscaped parklands and vistas of the 18th century, though the formal design at Hesleyside in Tynedale can still be traced under later alterations. The great landscape gardener, Lancelot 'Capability' Brown, was born at Kirkharle in 1715 and began his career as a gardener on the Kirkharle estate of the progressive landowner, Sir William Loraine. In Northumberland, Brown worked at Alnwick, Hesleyside and at Wallington, where he also created Rothley Lake for the Blacketts.

A leading figure in the landed society of mid-Georgian Northumberland was Lancelot Allgood of Nunwick, near Simonburn. The Allgoods had earlier been lawyers and agents to the Radcliffe Earls of Derwentwater, but had since become major landowners themselves. Lancelot, born in 1711 at Brandon White House, near Glanton, made the Grand Tour of France and Italy in 1736-38, and acquired Simonburn and other extensive estates when he married his relative, Jane

Gateway to Swinburne Castle

Allgood. In 1749 he swept away the small village of Nunwick to build the present mansion. A great 'improver', he developed the farms around Nunwick, improving the husbandry and enclosing moorland, and was a leading promoter of the turnpike road system. In 1745–46 he became high sheriff of Northumberland, and as a Tory with past family Jacobite connections Lancelot was particularly ardent in proving his loyalty and clamping down on Catholics and Jacobites. From 1748–53 he was M.P. for Northumberland and was knighted in 1760. In 1761 he was one of the county Deputy-Lieutenants when rioting broke out over compulsory ballotting for the county militia, and mobs seized and burnt the militia lists. At Hexham a crowd nearly 5,000 strong met the Deputy-Lieutenants and their soldiers, and violence broke out: 18 rioters and one officer were killed. Sir Lancelot and the other magistrates retreated to Newcastle, leaving his wife to face the local populace around Nunwick, which Jane calmly did and wrote to persuade Lancelot to come home 'or else they'll fancy they have banished you the country'. Like other leading landowners and county officials Sir Lancelot maintained a Newcastle house, and the accounts of the assembly rooms in the Groat Market note the attendance of Sir Lancelot with Mrs. and Miss Allgood on 2 May 1763 and 'tea for Sir Lancelot Allgood, 3s.'.

After mid-century the Percy family re-emerged to dominate county society. The 11th and last Earl's daughter married the Duke of Somerset, and her grand-daughter and heiress married Sir Hugh Smithson. Sir Hugh changed his surname to Percy, and was made Earl in 1750 and Duke of Northumberland in 1766. The Duke restored and rebuilt the ruinous Alnwick Castle in Gothic fashion, employing Robert Adam from 1760 to 1766. As well as the alterations to the castle (such as the building of several of the towers) and the interior decorations, the Duke also had the surroundings landscaped, and built the Gothic embellishments and follies like the Lion Bridge over the Aln, the observatory on Ratcheugh Crags, Brizlee Tower to the west of Alnwick, and the sham-medieval gate-tower of Pottersgate in Alnwick town itself. The Percies once again headed county society (indeed, in the early 19th century life at Alnwick was more like a princely court than the country house of an English aristocrat), and the Gothic style became the local fashion. Sir Lancelot Allgood built Gothic-style kennels at Nunwick, and in the 1770s Sir Francis Blake rebuilt Fowberry Tower, near Chatton, creating a particularly pleasant north front, and began his medieval castle on the cliff above Twizell Bridge, a project never completed because of Blake's bankruptcy.

Arms of Allgood

23. Netherwitton Hall, built in 1698 by the Thorntons, descendents of the medieval Newcastle merchant.

24. Seaton Sluice in 1778. Ships are lying in the old harbour and to the right a ship is coming through the New Cut of 1764.

25. Coal wagon and wagonway in about 1773, with staithes and a keel on the river behind.

26. Rimside Turnpike. The high stretch of the Newcastle-Wooler turnpike built in 1751 and abandoned in 1831.

At Craster, George Craster was adding Gothic battlements to the medieval tower in 1769, and building the Gothic archway over the road to Craster village, as well as building the present Georgian mansion on to the tower. The Craster family had survived the vicissitudes of border conflict and civil war, and a Stuart house had been added to the medieval tower between 1666 and 1675. After financial difficulties in the late 17th century, the family fortunes had improved. Between 1737 and 1757 the rents of the Craster estates in Northumberland and Durham doubled, and the family also gained wealth after an inheritance suit. Leading members of the family were absentees for the earlier part of the century: John Craster (1697–1763) was a lawyer who became an M.P. for a pocket-borough and a bencher of Gray's Inn. His son, George (1735–72) was a man of fashion, who became an officer in the Horse Guards (the purchase cost his father £2,000) and went on the Grand Tour with his wife in the 1760s. He and his wife continued to divide their time between Craster, London and Paris. The probate inventory at George's death in 1772 shows how the wealth of the Northumbrian gentry had increased. It includes Chippendale furniture, a large Turkish carpet, silk damask curtains, fine Holland sheets, a hand-painted tea-set of Sevres china, and many other luxury items, as well as George Craster's clothes, like his 'Crimson velvet suit with two pairs breeches, flower silk waistcoat with gold ground. Light-coloured suit, silver-laced'.

Craster Tower

In the early 19th century the classical Greek architectural style was introduced by Sir Charles Monck's Belsay Hall and, reinforced by the example of the 1830s planning of central Newcastle, it dominated for much of the century. John Dobson built country houses in the classical style at Mitford, Nunnykirk, Longhirst, and Meldon. But other styles retained some popularity, and at Lilburn Tower Dobson built a Tudor-style house and at Beaufront Castle, near Corbridge, a piece of grand Gothic. At Alnwick the new Gothic romanticism found expression during the 1850s in the work of the fourth Duke and the architect Salvin, who converted the lighter Gothic of Adam into the heavier style we see today. Later in Victoria's reign fewer new country houses were built, but at Cragside, near Rothbury, the industrialist, Lord Armstrong had Norman Shaw design a Wagnerian-cum-Tudor mansion that seems to have escaped from some German forest. Romantic in style, it was practical in operation: Armstrong had it lit by the new electric light of Joseph Swan, and generated the electricity by his own water-turbine. By 1900 the great era of country-house building was almost over, though modernising old castles was fashionable. In 1894 Armstrong restored Bamburgh Castle and in the early years of the new century Sir Edwin Lutyens converted the ruinous castle on Holy Island into a home for Edward Hudson, owner of *Country Life*.

Linden Hall

XIX Hanoverian Newcastle

Until the mid-18th century Newcastle remained largely confined within its medieval framework, and as late as the 1745 Rebellion the town walls were repaired for defence. After 1750, however, the pace of growth and change in the town, as in the county, quickened. In 1763 the wall along the Quayside was pulled down, and the corporation began to light the main streets at night with oil lamps, and set up a night patrol. New residential squares for the wealthy began to change the character of the town. As early as 1736 Bourne noted the movement away from the Close and Sandhill to houses in Pilgrim Street and Westgate, described as 'a Street more retired than any other in this Town; there being no Artificers or Mechanicks in this Street, nor any Market. It is chiefly inhabited by the Clergy and Gentry'. In the 1780s Clavering Place (where Clavering House, built *c.* 1784, still survives) was built on the site of the White Friars, and Hanover Square extended, creating a pleasant quarter with fine views up the river. Now much changed, it was described by R. J. Charleton in the 1880s as 'a quiet old-fashioned nook . . . looking more like part of some sleepy cathedral city than of a busy manufacturing town'. Charlotte Square was built near Blackfriars and outside the town walls new houses were constructed in lower Northumberland Street, backed by extensive gardens. Off Northumberland Street the elegant rows of Saville Place and Saville Row were built about 1788.

Clavering House

Traffic coming over the Tyne bridge still had to pull up the tortuous Side to reach the upper town, and access from Pilgrim Street was difficult. The lower part of the Lort Burn in the Side had been paved over in the 1690s, but the rest of the Burn remained a nauseous sewer and tip in the centre of the town. Plans were developed by the corporation in the 1760s, but they were delayed by the crisis of 1771. On Sunday night, 17 November 1771, an intense rainstorm to the west raised the level of the Tyne dramatically, and all the Tyne bridges, except Corbridge, were swept away, including the old bridge at Newcastle (Plate 27) and the Close and Sandhill were flooded. The new bridge cost the corporation over £30,000, and it was not until its completion in 1781 that other improvements could be considered. Between 1784 and 1789 parts of the Lort were filled in, and Dean Street was built over it. At the top a new cross road, Mosley Street, was constructed to join Pilgrim Street to the main centre of the town,

Window ironwork, Dean Street

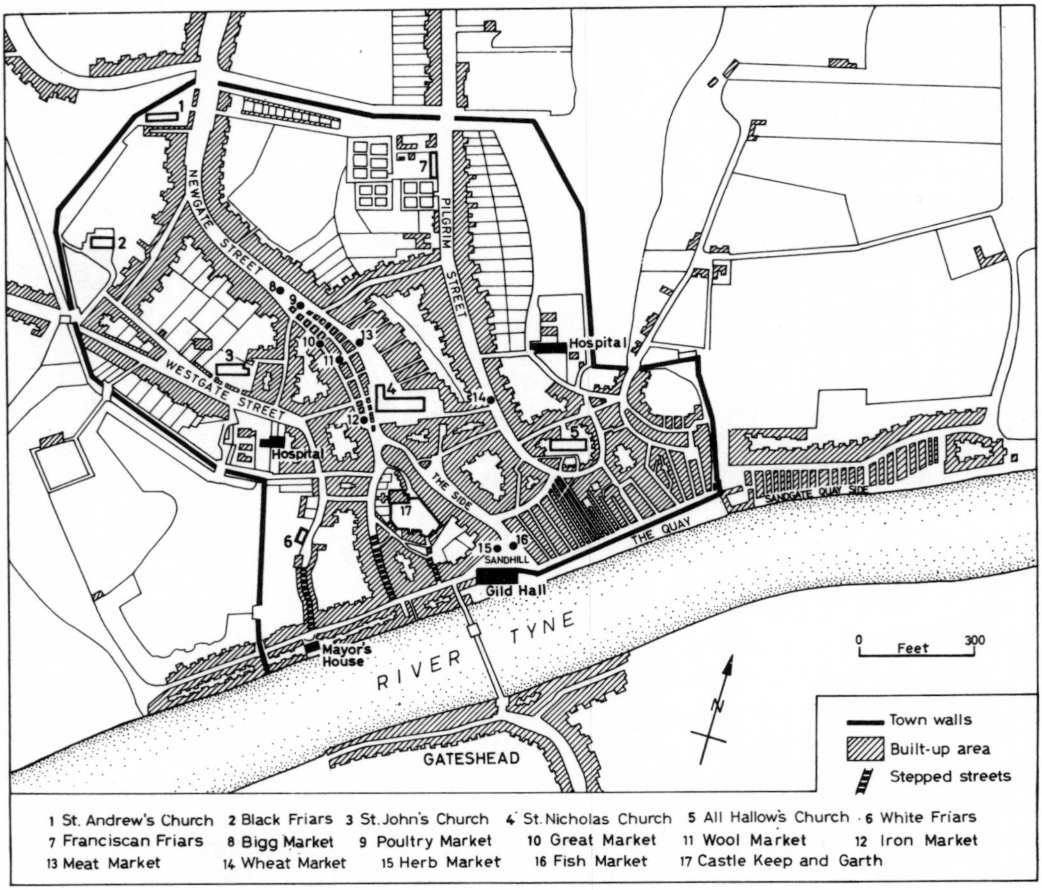

9. Newcastle in 1723

and traffic-flow was now easier between the bridge and the Bigg and Groat Markets. In Mosley Street a Theatre Royal was built in 1788, and in 1810 the street was extended by building Collingwood Street to join Westgate, and fashionable display windows were put in the shops in these streets.

There were numerous other improvements. In the east of the town the elegant St. Ann's church, now rather neglected by visitors, was built in 1768 to cater for the Sandgate populace. The old All Saints' church was pulled down and the present church, by David Stephenson, completed by 1796. In 1783–4 a new White Cross in Newgate Street and Cale Cross in the Side were built by Sir Matthew White Ridley. New Bridge Street was built in 1812 and between 1795 and 1811 the gates of the medieval town were pulled down, except for Newgate, which survived until 1823.

The Georgian improvements were not just in the physical fabric of the town, but also in the whole social and cultural life of the wealthier sections of Newcastle society. In 1736 a series of public concerts was started by Charles Avison, organist at St. Nicholas's. The gatherings of town and county society that were held during Race Week became more frequent, first during the Assize Weeks and then more regularly. From 1736 to 1776 the assembly rooms for receptions, balls and card-playing were in Ridley Court, off the Groat Market. The stocks of the assembly rooms in December 1762 included 26 packs of cards and a wine-cellar of 10 bottles of Lisbon, six Port, 16 Mountain, and six Rhenish, though tea was the main drink taken. Lord Chancellor Eldon, previously John Scott of Newcastle, recollected these assemblies: '. . . so we always danced from the large room, across the stairhead, and into the other room. Then you know, Ellen, that was very convenient, for the small room was a snug one to flirt in. We always engaged our partners for the next ball, and from year to year. We were very constant'. In 1776 the new Assembly Rooms in Westgate were opened.

Newcastle had had a newspaper (the *Newcastle Courant*) since 1712, and by 1802 there were five. It became a centre of printing and publishing (especially religious tracts and children's books), culminating in the illustrations of Thomas Bewick, who published his *History of British Birds* in 1797 and 1804. Education also improved: in 1749 the Free Grammar School of Queen Elizabeth, founded in 1540 and refounded in the Elizabethan charter of 1600, was at a low ebb, with very few pupils, but the new headmaster, Hugh Moises, revitalised it, and from it came Lord Eldon, his brother, William (later Lord Stowell), Lord Collingwood, and others. There was also a number of good private academies, such as that started by Dr. Charles Hutton in Westgate in 1760. The growing professional and middle classes in the town—teachers, manufacturers, clergymen like William Turner the Unitarian minister, and the medical men who were replacing the old barber-surgeon craft guild—began a number of literary, scientific and humanitarian societies. In 1793 the Literary and Philosophical Society was founded, and in 1813 the Society of Antiquaries.

Apart from providing building and labouring work, many of the civic improvements must have meant little to the Newcastle poor and working classes clustered in shabby housing in Sandgate and the lanes round Newgate. The town population grew to 28,000 in the 18th century, and there were acute problems of poverty and disease. The seasonal nature of the coal trade left the keelmen unemployed for three to four months each year, and many were unable to claim poor relief since they had not been born locally and their seasonal

White Cross, Newgate Street

Cale Cross, the Side

employment did not qualify them as residents. Severe winters could lead to great distress, and when the acute winter of 1740 was followed by steep rises in bread-grain prices the urban mob rioted on 9 June, and the corporation agreed to regulate prices. A fortnight later rumours spread that ships were going to take the grain to other ports to get higher prices, and many shops refused to sell at the controlled prices. On 25 June a large crowd marched to the Guildhall. In a clash with a town official, a pitman was killed, and the crowd attacked the Guildhall, ejecting the officials, throwing stones 'like cannon shot' through the windows, ransacking the town records, and taking nearly £1,400 out of the 'public hutch' or chest. The following evening troops arrived from Alnwick and arrested 40 rioters, seven of whom were later transported.

Society's outlook was that poverty and great inequality were inevitable—and even radicals accepted this—but within the norms of the age the ruling group in the town often tried to relieve poverty and suffering. During the severe winter of 1728 the Newcastle magistrates collected £362 18s. 0d. (£362.90p) for the relief of the poor, and in the winter of 1740 Blackett gave £350 to the needy (and became known as Father of the Poor), while Alderman Ridley allowed the poor to take coal from his heaps. During the 18th century new almshouses were set up in addition to those already in the Manors, and several charity schools were founded. All these charities gave some help, but when John Wesley came to Newcastle in 1742 his message of religious salvation found a ready audience amongst many of Newcastle's poor, and a Methodist meeting-house was set up in 1745. The improvements in medical knowledge were reflected in the Infirmary for the poor founded in 1751, the Lying-in (maternity) hospital in 1760 and the Dispensary for free medicines in 1778. There was also charitable self-help from the poor themselves: working the keels was punishing, and there were many older men no longer fit, so in 1699 the keelmen organised a fund (based on a deduction from wages), and the Keelmen's Hospital was built to house 50 ex-keelmen, and the fund also provided out-relief. The Newcastle ruling group were, as ever, quick to sense any threat: the keelmen's fund was administered by the Hostmen in case the keelmen should use it to finance industrial action.

One aspect of Newcastle life which showed few signs of change was its government. Although the Hostmen had lost their monopoly control of the Tyneside coal industry in the later 17th century (see Chapter XX), the oligarchy of leading Newcastle-based mine-owners, merchants and coal-shippers continued to rule the town under its old constitution. A small group of families intermarried and handed down town office like family heirlooms. The group altered as old families declined, or became county gentry, and new merchants established themselves, often marrying the daughters of the oligarchy. In the first half of the Hanoverian period the dominant family were the Blacketts, who had purchased Newe House in Pilgrim Street as their town residence. Coalowners, landowners, merchants, and lead-mine owners, the Blacketts played a leading role until the 1770s. Sir Walter Calverley Blackett was mayor five times between 1734 and 1771 and M.P. in seven parliaments.

The great Clayton dynasty in the town was founded by Nathaniel Clayton, son of a Yorkshire rector. A merchant, he was sheriff in 1715 and mayor in 1725 and 1738. His son, William, was mayor in 1750, 1755, and 1763, and William's close relative, Robert, was mayor in 1804, 1812, and 1817. Robert's brother, Nathaniel, purchased the office of town clerk for £2,100 in 1785 and held it until 1822. Robert's sons were both sheriffs, in 1817 and 1818, and Nathaniel's famous son John succeeded his father as town clerk in 1822 and held the office until 1867, over 150 years after the first Nathaniel became sheriff.

All Saints' church

Nicholas Ridley was the son of an old landed family at Willimoteswick in the Tyne valley, who became a merchant, sheriff in 1682, and mayor in 1706. His son, Richard, was mayor in 1713, and his grandson, William (who was mayor in 1733, 1751 and 1759, and M.P. from 1747 to 1774) married the heiress of Sir Matthew White of Blagdon, another leading oligarch. Their son, Sir Matthew White Ridley was mayor in 1774, 1782 and 1791, and M.P. from 1774 to 1812, and the Ridleys are still at Blagdon and prominent in county politics. Other leading families in the later Georgian period were the Brandlings, Cooksons, Surtees, and the Bells of Woolsington.

XX Mining Expansion and Industrial Growth

Tyneside keelman

In the later 17th century the Newcastle Hostmen lose their control of Tyneside coal production, though not the coal traffic on the river. The disruptions of the Civil War led to non-Hostmen acquiring coal interests and an increasing willingness by non-coalowning Hostmen to act as agents for their coal. The Hostmen became differentiated into a large group of 'fitters' who ran the keel traffic and marketed for the coal-owners, and a small number who now regarded themselves primarily as coalowners. The Liddells, for example, were royalist Hostmen and became Durham-based coalowners like the Bowes and Wortleys, and took little part in Newcastle guilds or politics. A few, though, like the Blacketts, retained their Newcastle base. The leading coalowners periodically formed cartels to manage output, notably the 'Grand Allies' of Liddell, Bowes and Wortley in 1726, and the 'Vend' after 1771.

These changes were also related to the exhaustion and drainage problems of old pits. Elswick pit was flooded in 1680. A 1689 petition claimed that 'the coal-pits nearest the water are almost quite exhausted and decayed'. New pits started up away from the river, mainly in north-west Durham, where coal from shallow seams was transported along wooden wagonways to the Tyne. These new wagonways (Plate 25) were costly to build and also meant paying landowners for expensive 'wayleaves'. Coalowners even tried to block their rivals by buying negative wayleaves, and in the 1720s Newcastle coalowner Richard Ridley persuaded Newcastle corporation to refuse a wayleave from Heaton colliery to William Cotesworth the Gateshead coalowner.

The invention of Newcomen's steam or 'atmospheric' engine in 1710 eased the drainage problem. By the 1720s north Tyneside pits were re-opening and expanding, with wagonways to the river. Collieries were opened at Byker, Jesmond, Heaton, Wylam, and further north at Holywell Main, and later along the south edge of the 90-fathom dyke or fault north-east of Newcastle, such as Longbenton pit in 1735. By 1767 Longbenton had the largest output on north Tyneside, followed by Throckley and Holywell Main, west of Newcastle. On the coast, a wagonway had been constructed from Plessey pits to Blyth before 1710, and its route can still be traced. In 1722 Matthew White and Richard Ridley acquired these estates and developed Blyth as a coal and small commercial port. At Seaton Sluice the Delavals

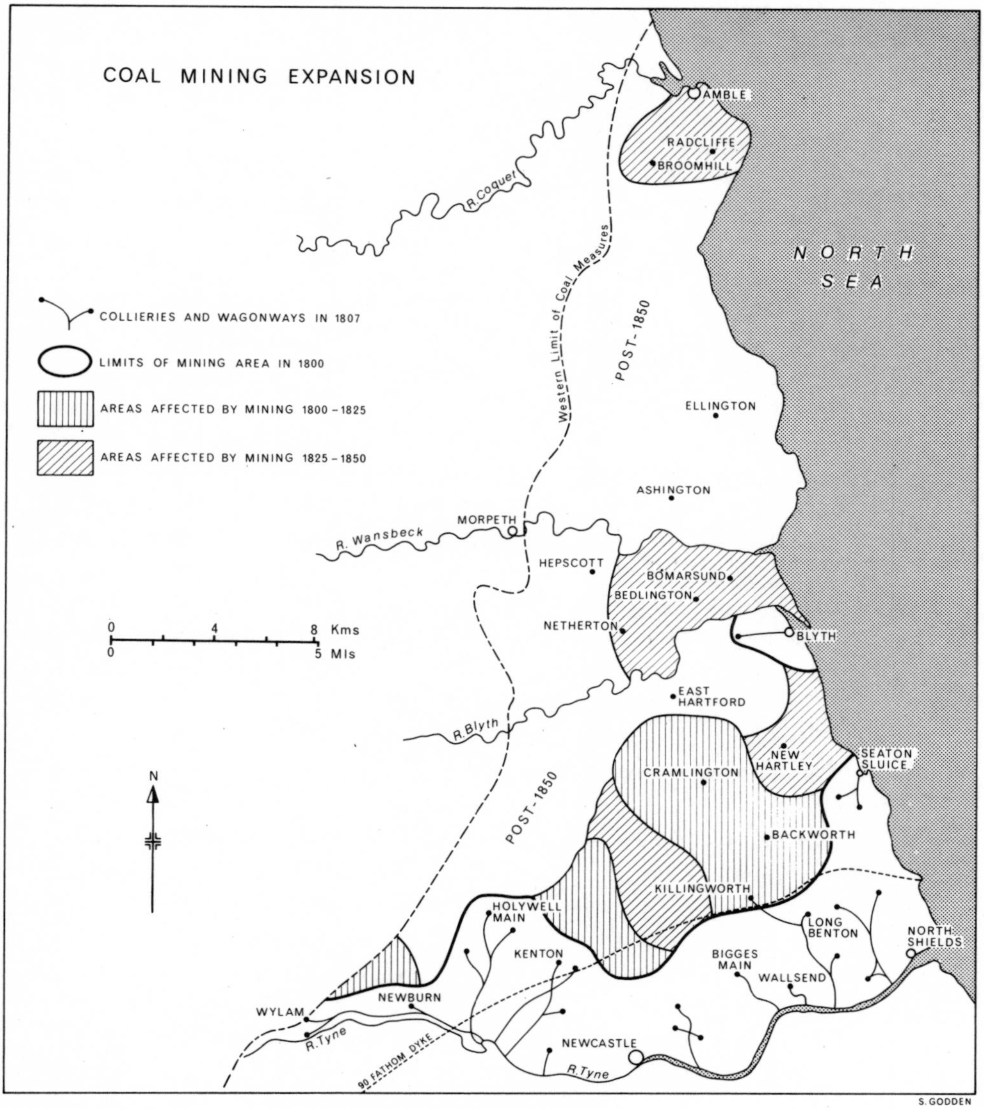
COAL MINING EXPANSION
COLLIERIES AND WAGONWAYS IN 1807
LIMITS OF MINING AREA IN 1800
AREAS AFFECTED BY MINING 1800 - 1825
AREAS AFFECTED BY MINING 1825 - 1850
NORTH SEA
AMBLE
RADCLIFFE
BROOMHILL
R. Coquet
Western Limit of Coal Measures
POST-1850
ELLINGTON
ASHINGTON
MORPETH
R. Wansbeck
HEPSCOTT
BOMARSUND
BEDLINGTON
NETHERTON
BLYTH
0 4 8 Kms
0 5 Mls
EAST HARTFORD
R. Blyth
N
CRAMLINGTON
NEW HARTLEY
SEATON SLUICE
POST-1850
BACKWORTH
KILLINGWORTH
HOLYWELL MAIN
KENTON
LONG BENTON
NORTH SHIELDS
BIGGES MAIN
WALLSEND
WYLAM
NEWBURN
R. Tyne
90 FATHOM DYKE
NEWCASTLE
R. Tyne
S. GODDEN

10. Coalmining Expansion

expanded their coal operations, especially after 1750, and 1761–4 excavated a new harbour entrance through solid rock to give better facilities (Plate 24). In 1777 177 ships left the harbour with coal.

The introduction of gunpowder to sink deeper shafts, and cast-iron cylinders (in place of brass) for larger pumping engines, allowed the mining of the deep, rich coal-seams in the Wallsend basin. Walker pit was sunk in 1758, drained by three engines, and reached coal at 600 feet. Willington pit followed in 1775, Wallsend in the 1780s, after several explosions, Bigge's Main in 1784, and Percy Main in 1796–9. By 1800 the main output was coming from these Wallsend pits, which were convenient for shipping coal direct from coal-staithes into the colliers through 'spouts' (Plate 25), and later coal-drops (Plate 30) which lessened breakage. This direct loading gradually diminished employment in the keel trade. Further Wallsend basin pits were developed after 1800; one north of Bigge's Main was the Craster pit, for the Craster family owned land in Longbenton. However, in 1802 the Grand Allies sank Killingworth pit, and opened up a new mining area north of the 90-fathom dyke, where the steep dip of the beds had prevented earlier working, and after 1820 many miners moved to this area, with further pits at Burradon and Backworth.

Explosive gases in the deep pits caused heavy loss of life, and lighting was a problem. Even the feeble light of phosphorescent fish was used, and at Wallsend a mirror reflected light into one gaseous shaft. The Davy and Stephenson safety lamps after 1815 should have helped, but just led to working still deeper seams and dangerous shafts: more output, but no more safety.

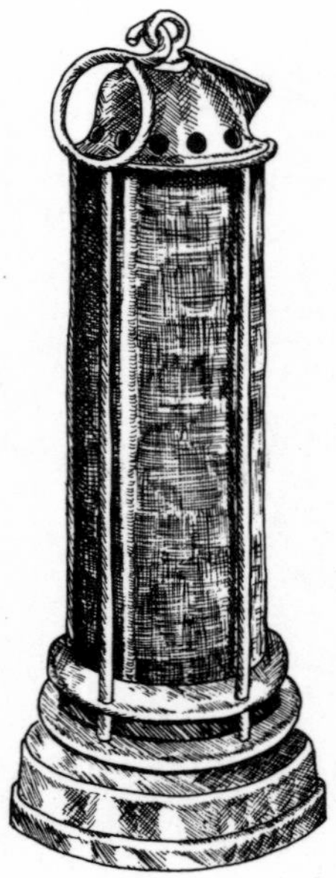

Stephenson safety lamp

The wooden wagonways were gradually converted to iron rails; the first stretch on Tyneside was from Walker to the staithes in 1797. Steam-locomotives were also introduced. The Cornish mining engineer, Trevithick, visited Newcastle in 1804 with details of his locomotive, and Christhopher Blackett ordered one, but never took delivery of it, possibly because his 5-mile wagonway from Wylam to Scotswood was still wooden until 1808. When Blackett contacted Trevithick again in 1809, he was no longer interested. However, in 1813 Blackett's manager, William Hedley, designed a similar engine (the *Puffing Billy*), which ran for many years. On the Kenton wagonway, a design by Blenkinsop was tried, based on a rack-and-pinion system rather than Trevithick's smooth wheels. At Killingworth the Grand Allies asked George Stephenson to design a locomotive. Stephenson's designs led to a number of engines on Tyneside wagonways by the early 1820s, but the big breakthrough came with the public demonstration of the Stockton and Darlington railway in 1825.

The railway allowed further mining expansion north of the 90-fathom dyke. North of Backworth the household High Main coal deteriorates and the Low Main coal suitable for steam-production dominates. The demand for steam-coal in industry and transport was growing and formed the basis for future coal-mining expansion. Export duties on coal were reduced in 1831, and eventually abolished, and the Northumberland coalfield became a major exporter: exports from Newcastle rose from 157,000 tons in 1828 to 476,000 tons in 1837. The railways also threatened the Tyneside coalowners, however, by bringing competition from areas like South Durham, and the rights of way given by the railway Acts destroyed lucrative wayleave rents. Coal cartel members opposed new lines like the South Durham Railway in 1836, when each contributed one per cent. of royalties and wayleave rents to the fighting fund. The Duke of Northumberland's £180 18s. 4d. (£180.92p) meant he was getting £18,000 a year in such rents. In the mid-1840s though, they gave up this battle, and the cartel collapsed.

Coal was not the only mining industry in Northumberland. The lead mines of the north Pennines, on the moors where Northumberland, Durham and Cumberland met, had been worked in the medieval period, and in the late 17th century there was a revival of mining activity on a larger scale. During the 18th century output from Alston Moor and Allendale increased with improved techniques of smelting and mining, driving long tunnels or adits into the hills. The main mining groups in these areas were the London Lead Company (who leased the ex-Radcliffe lands from the Greenwich Hospital Commissioners) and the Blackett-Beaumont family, who had acquired Allendale from the Fenwicks in 1689. In good periods leadmining was very profitable, and around 1820 the Blackett-Beaumonts were making as much as £60,000 a year.

Transporting the lead ore from these remote mines was difficult. The ore was pulverised and washed on site, then carried on pack-horses to the lead smelters. These were built on the lower land below the moors, and when the London Lead Co. built a smelter in 1706 they made careful calculations of the best location, finding it was 7s. (35p) a fother of lead cheaper to smelt at Whitfield than at Ryton-on-Tyne, where coal would be cheaper. In the Northumbrian foothills smelting mills were built at Allen (1692), Whitfield (1706), Dukesfield (pre-1725), and Langley (1767).

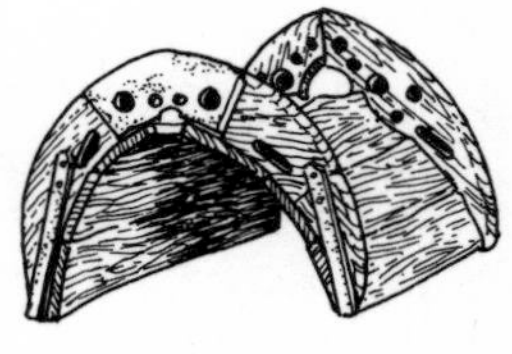

Pack-saddle for lead

Industrial growth in this period from 1700 to 1840 took several forms. As in many other parts of England there was investment (especially after 1750) in rural industries often using water-power: the paper mills at Haughton on the North Tyne in 1788, and

Netherwitton mill

Fourstones on the South Tyne, the woollen mills at Mitford, Newtown (Rothbury) and elsewhere, the cotton mill at Netherwitton, and the iron foundries at Bedlington and at Acklington Park on the Coquet. These mills and foundries reflected the growing market in Northumberland and especially in Tyneside.

More distinctive and important was the industrial growth on Tyneside related to the coal trade. The long-established glass industry, using local coals and sands brought as ballast by colliers, expanded, especially at the end of the century. In 1772 there were 16 Tyneside glassworks, by 1812 there were thirty. These produced a wide variety of glassware, from glass bottles and cheap soda glass to the delicate enamelled glassware of the Beilbys. On North Tyneside the main centres were at Ouseburn, Closegate in Newcastle, and at Lemington, opened in 1780, where a glass cone survives. At Seaton Sluice the Delavals began a glassworks in the 1760s, and in 1776 they shipped 840,000 bottles from their harbour. A group of inter-connected industries sprang up around glassmaking. Glass required soda and potash, and in 1797 William and John Losh leased the brine from Walker pit and were soon using the new Le Blanc process to make alkali. Other firms came in, and by 1850 alkali was second to coal in shipments from the Tyne, much of it going to the textile districts. There was also soap and paint making, and all the new chemical production created pollution problems on Tyneside.

The second growth sector was the iron industry, making products for the coal industry and coal shipping. Until 1800 the iron foundries made nails, anchors, chains and cylinders for pumping engines. Bedlington ironworks was famous for its nails. With demand for iron rails and steam-locomotives the industry expanded, and after 1800 more foundries were set up along the Tyne, replacing water-driven hammers with the new Watt steam-engines. Losh, Wilson, and Bell started their Walker ironworks in 1807. Cast-iron rails were brittle and cracked under locomotives, and in the 1820s Bedlington acquired a new reputation for malleable iron rails, using the rolling-mill installed in 1809. The first Tyne steamboat was the *Perseverance,* which began a Newcastle to North Shields service in 1814, and the need for both steamboat and locomotive engines stimulated the beginnings of an engineering industry. Stephenson set up a works, and in 1817 Robert Hawthorn formed his engine works at Forth Banks, Newcastle, and in 1822 installed steam-power to drive his machines. Until the 1830s most of the pig iron was imported, or scrap iron used, though Bedlington had tried smelting rather unsuccessfully in the 18th century and there was smelting at Lemington-on-Tyne after 1795. In the 1830s and 1840s blast-furnaces were built to use coal and local ore at Ridsdale in Redesdale (1839), and Hareshaw, near Bellingham (1841), and on the Tyne at Wylam (1836), and using imported ore, at the Walker works in 1842. Despite the growth of the Tyneside iron and chemical-related industries after 1800, in 1840 most of the factories were still small, and Tyneside was not an industrialised region like the textile districts of Lancashire and Yorkshire with their large factory employment.

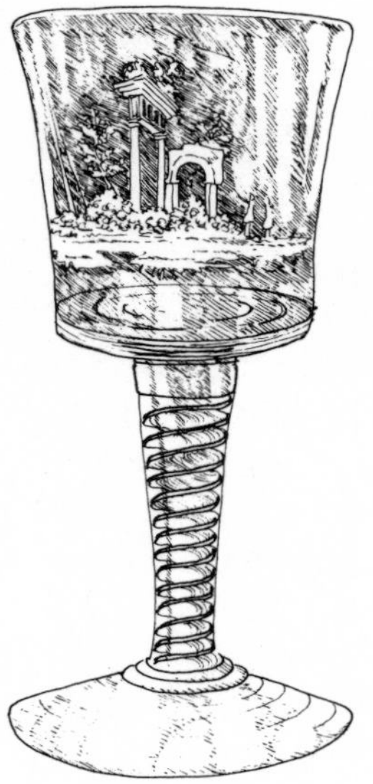

Beilby glass

XXI Turnpikes and Railways

Stage-coach

From the Roman occupation to the mid-18th century no properly surveyed and constructed roads were built in Northumberland. Movement was by way of 'routes' rather than proper roads. From Norman times the Great North Road from Newcastle to Alnwick and Berwick was important, but it was not a constructed road. Travel on these routes was often difficult; as early as the reign of Henry II we hear of two monks who accompanied the King complaining of the state of Northumberland's roads.

Some of the routes are not followed by major roads today. The drove roads over the Scottish border have already been discussed in Chapter XII. Another important route, probably originating in Anglo-Saxon times, ran north from Tynemouth to Bedlington, passing through Chirton, Murton, Earsdon, Stickley, and Horton, and then north up the coast to Bamburgh and Lindisfarne. Linking church estates, it was used in 1069 by monks fleeing with Cuthbert's body from William. Edward I travelled along it three times. Maintenance was a problem: in 1326 Sir Robert de la Val agreed with the Prior of Tynemouth to repair the road over his moor between Stickley and Holywell, which was so deep and muddy that carts could not move along it. Today, local roads follow its route from Tynemouth to Bedlington, except between Murton and Earsdon, where its course was probably the path through the fields.

Estates at Embleton belonged to Merton College, Oxford, and the record of a journey by one of the college bursars to superintend the harvest and tithes in 1464 has survived. He travelled north to Newcastle, then via Ponteland (where there was a college living) to Rothbury, and across Bolton Moors to Alnwick and Embleton. The bursar paid twopence to a guide for directing him across the difficult Bolton Moors.

Roads did not improve. In 1559 the Earl of Northumberland, commenting on the main road to Berwick, said 'the cattle of this country are so little and so weak, and *the way so deep,* that they can scarce draw an empty carriage'. The state of the roads became more important as carriages replaced horses, and the movement of agricultural and industrial products in bulk more significant. In 1658 there was a coach from London to Edinburgh which took thirteen days, six from Newcastle. Since the first sprung carriage was built in 1754, it must have been an uncomfortable fortnight. A revived service began in 1712 and lasted until 1729. An advertisement in the *Newcastle Courant* for 6 January 1728 reads, 'Lost, between Alnwick and Felton Bridge, from the Stage Coach, a pair of Leather baggs, wherein were some wearing linen, coffee, coffee cups, and other things: Whoever brings them to Mrs. Smith, Post-Mistress at Morpeth, shall have a guinea reward, and no questions asked'.

Black Bull, Morpeth

Maintenance of the roads fell on each local parish. So in 1701 the Quarter Sessions record 'John Coatsworth, esq., presents the highway in the Thorns loaning att a place called Shordon Sike to be Foundrous and ought to be repaired by the inhabitants of the township of Anick' (near Corbridge). This fell particularly hard on parishes along the North Road, who were also expected to supply carts for military traffic.

The solution was a commercial road-system. By raising subscription investment, capital was obtained to build proper roads, and this was recouped by tolls on users of these turnpike roads. Such roads had existed further south since the 1660s, but the first in the north was that from Newcastle to near Berwick in 1746. A spate of these roads was built in the succeeding years. Most were on existing routes, but the Military Road was built largely along the line of the Roman Wall, because General Wade had found he could not drag his guns further than Hexham on his way to Carlisle in the 1745 Rebellion. For the most part though, 'the turnpike was the landowner's creation for the landowner's use' (W. G. Dodds), and the same names of improving landlords, such as the Allgoods, Blacketts, Middletons, and Swinburnes, keep appearing in the Acts setting up the turnpikes.

These turnpikes were made of packed stone-chips. Whinstone was the best material. Henry Wilson, surveyor of the Alnmouth-Hexham road in 1851, noted 'Whin is very much more beneficial than limestone as where the carriage is so heavy limestone wears away so quickly'. In setting tolls the plan was to exempt very local agricultural traffic and tap long-distance commercial traffic. Several routes retain their turnpike form, except for the surfacing. A fine example is the Alnmouth-Hexham road through Alnwick and Rothbury, turnpiked in 1751. It was known as the Corn Road because its main trade was the export of corn from central and south-west Northumberland through the port of Alnmouth. Another good stretch is the Morpeth-Elsdon turnpike, west of Longwitton. The Newcastle-Wooler road, built in the 1750s, originally ran over Rimside Moor but was diverted east to the present line in 1831. The old turnpike across the top of Rimside still survives as a bridleway, and along it the stone surface, side-drains, bridges and boundaries can still

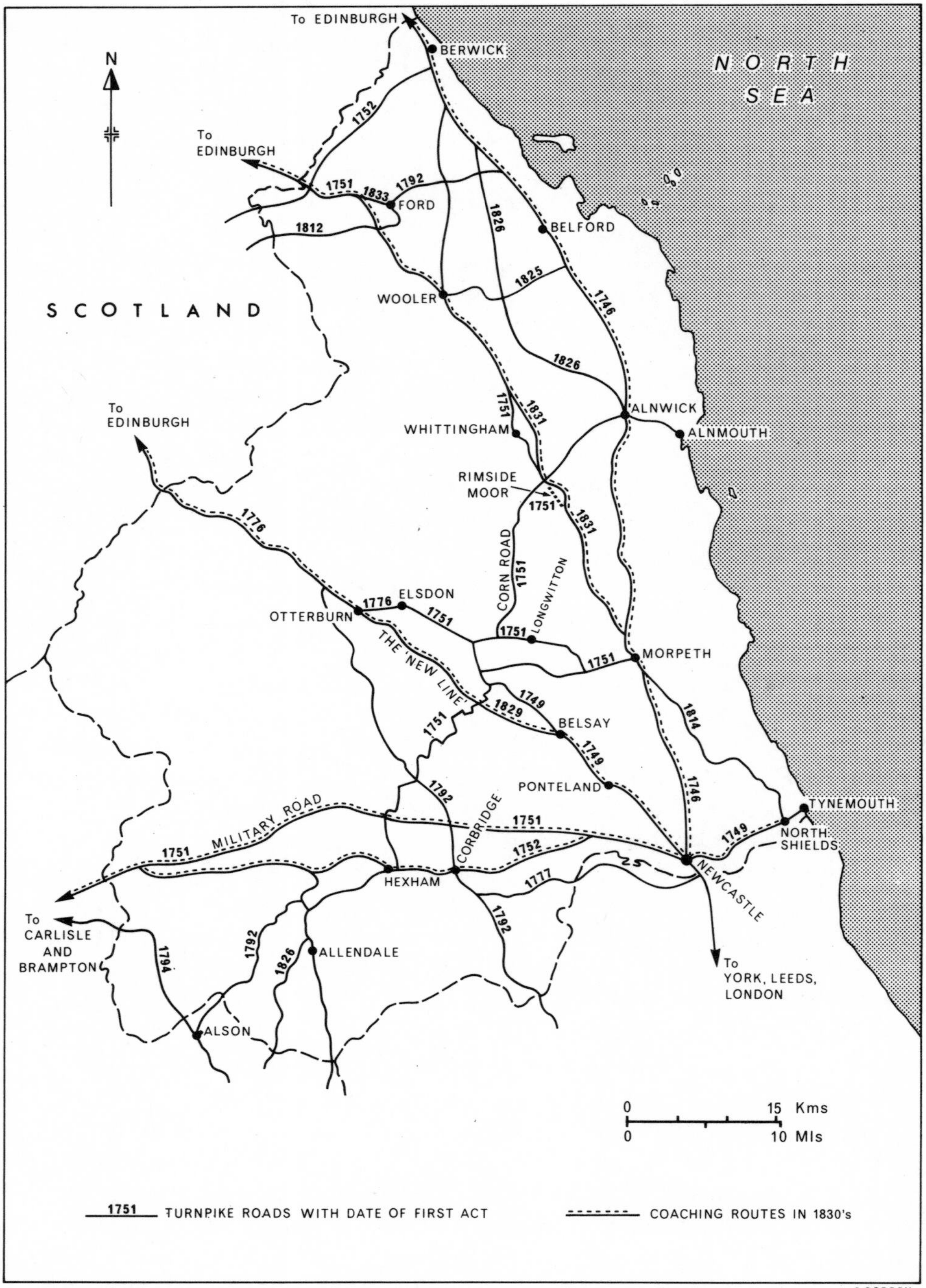

11. Turnpike Roads

27. The Last of the Old Tyne Bridge, 1771. An oil painting by Wilson Hepple, now in the Shipley Gallery, Gateshead.

28. Newcastle Quayside in 1820.

29. North Shields in 1825, with the collier fleet at anchor. In the far distance are the New Quay and the Northumberland Arms, scene of the 1819 shooting and riot.

30. Coal drops and colliers at Wallsend in 1844.

be traced (Plate 26), ascending to the lonely ruins of the *Swinburne Arms,* an old coaching stop, in the wood of Rimside.

These turnpikes led to the growth of coaching traffic in the 1750s. In 1763 there was a weekly coach to Edinburgh along the Rimside route from the *Bull* and the *Post-Boy* in the Bigg Market at Newcastle. By 1784 there were six coaches a week from the *Turk's Head*, and in 1811 the *Turf* in Collingwood Street had over eight coaches leaving each day to various places. Competition became intense between operators and routes. At the height of the coaching era, the 1820s, John Croall's 'Chevy Chase' ran to Edinburgh on the Otterburn route, James Redford's 'The High Flyer' took the Wooler road, and 'The Union' took the Great North Road. Important coaching inns and prosperity grew up at the stops on these routes at Morpeth, Alnwick, Belford, and out in the country. A good example is the *Castle Inn* at Whittingham, where the winter travellers could recover from the bitter ride through wind and snow across Rimside Moor.

Although these turnpikes were a major aid in improving agriculture, they could also hinder, for, like railways and motorways after them, they let goods in as well as out. John Hodgson, writing in 1827, noted the problems of farming in Redesdale: 'Its contiguity to the fine corn lands of Scotland, and a turnpike road through it, have been the means of introducing meal and flour into it at a lower price than they can, upon an average of years, be produced for on its own lands. Hence fewer ploughs are used here of late years than formerly were'.

For bulk transport canals were superior to roads, but no canals were built in Northumberland because the concentration of industrial activity on the coast and the navigable Tyne meant coastal shipping was available. Indeed, it was this access to cheap sea-transport that had given the North-east its lead over inland coalfields. The only seriously projected canal was one from Newcastle to Maryport, to export Tyneside coal to Ulster and the west coast and move linen and cotton goods to the east coast for shipment. In the 1790s William Chapman surveyed a line west to Haydon Bridge through Corbridge, Beaufront and St. John Lee, with an incredible number of locks. Rival routes south of the Tyne were outlined by Sutcliffe and Dodd, but for all routes local opposition always outweighted support.

The serious challenge to the turnpikes (and to smaller-scale east-coast shipping) came with the railway. George Stephenson, a local engineer from Ovingham, built his first passenger railway from Stockton to Darlington in 1825. Initially some were sceptical of the whole idea. One writer in the *Tyne Mercury* in 1824 said: 'What person would ever think of paying anything to be conveyed from

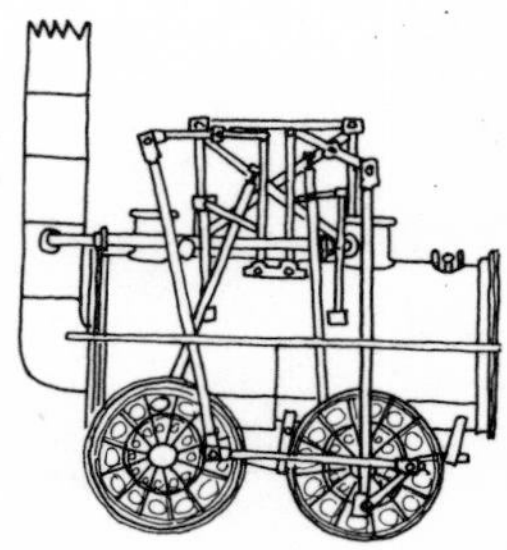

Stephenson's Locomotion

Silhouette of James Losh

Hexham to Newcastle in something like a coal-waggon, upon a dreary waggon-way, and to be dragged for the greater part of the distance by a roaring steam engine? The thing is too ridiculous to dwell upon, especially as we know that a person may come from Hexham in three hours by a coach, and for three or four shillings'. The new railway was popular, however. James Losh, who had been a promoter of the canal, became chairman of the Newcastle-Carlisle railway company, and employed Chapman as one of the engineers. The Blaydon-Hexham section was opened in May 1835 and the full route in 1839. The line from London reached Gateshead in 1844, and the construction of the High Level Bridge across the Tyne in 1849, and the Royal Border Bridge at Berwick enabled the 'Railway King' George Hudson to link up all the North-east. In succeeding decades the railways penetrated throughout Northumberland: the Wansbeck line to Scots Gap in 1862 and the Alnwick-Cornhill line in 1887.

As late as the 1830s new turnpike routes like the Belsay-Otterburn line were being constructed, but the coming of the railway rapidly damaged the turnpikes by attracting away both passenger and commercial traffic. By 1838 coachowners were asking for tax relief because of railway competition. William Robb looked back later: 'There was a much greater traffic between Newcastle and Carlisle by way of the Military Road, which, with the numerous carts often conveying large quantities of cotton yarn from Lancashire to Newcastle for shipment to the Baltic, and many country carriers as well, was not the desolate and dismal route it now is'. The last G.P.O. mail-coach to Edinburgh ran in July 1847, and after that the trains strangled the life out of coaching, which was dead by 1860. In the years to 1880 the various turnpike trusts were wound up, and road maintenance passed to the county authorities.

Though the railway brought improved communications its benefits to rural Northumberland were very mixed. The national rail network facilitated regional specialisation and local producers could not compete with cheaper imports to the region. Many of the county's smaller agricultural industries, harbours and market towns contracted or died. As the railways killed off local industries and motor transport came into being, so the tide of railway profitability turned and retreated. The Alnwick-Cornhill line lasted only until 1935. Traffic returned to the roads, and only a few miles from the fossilised turnpike on Rimside, past the foundations of the Roman Devil's Causeway, stands the derelict viaduct of the Alnwick line at Edlingham.

XXII *The Building of Central Newcastle*

Richard Grainger

The Georgian improvements in Newcastle left two parts of the town untouched: the old slums and chares of Sandgate and the Quayside, and the 12 acres of land belonging to the Newe House and Nun's Field in the upper town between Pilgrim Street and Newgate. The latter area had been offered to the town after Sir Walter Blackett's death in 1777, but the corporation had not purchased it. Instead it was bought by a wealthy builder, George Anderson, who re-named it Anderson Place. It remained unchanged until building contractor Richard Grainger, aided by architect John Dobson and town clerk John Clayton, developed the site in the 1830s to make Newcastle, in the words of architectural historian Nikolaus Pevsner, 'the best designed Victorian town in England and indeed the best designed large city in England altogether'.

Grainger, born in a poor family in 1797, became a builder's apprentice, but rapidly built up his own construction business, helped by £5,000 dowry from his wife. A thrusting entrepreneur, he built a series of residential blocks in the town: Higham Place in 1819-20, Eldon Square and large sections of the new Blackett Street in 1824-26, and Leazes Crescent and Terrace in 1829-34. In 1831-32 he built the Royal Arcade in Pilgrim Street, intending it as a new corn exchange, but the town corporation did not agree, and Grainger had to use it as a commercial and shopping centre, which did not succeed because of its distance from the town centre. Until 1834 Grainger was a builder of individual blocks. However, in 1831 George Anderson died, and the possibility of purchase arose, and in 1834 Grainger presented his comprehensive development plan to the town council. John Dobson, the architect, had put forward such plans in 1825, suggesting a large tree-lined square focussing on a new Mansion House and Guildhall, but whilst he got nowhere the more dynamic Richard Grainger was persuasive. The corporation had apparently already discussed improvements in 1832, and close co-operation with them was essential, so Grainger's legal adviser, John Fenwick, advised him to move his account to the solicitor's firm run by John Clayton, the town clerk, an interesting reflection on the ethics of town government. Clayton became Grainger's advocate and adviser, and the scheme was adopted remarkably quickly. Grainger put his plan

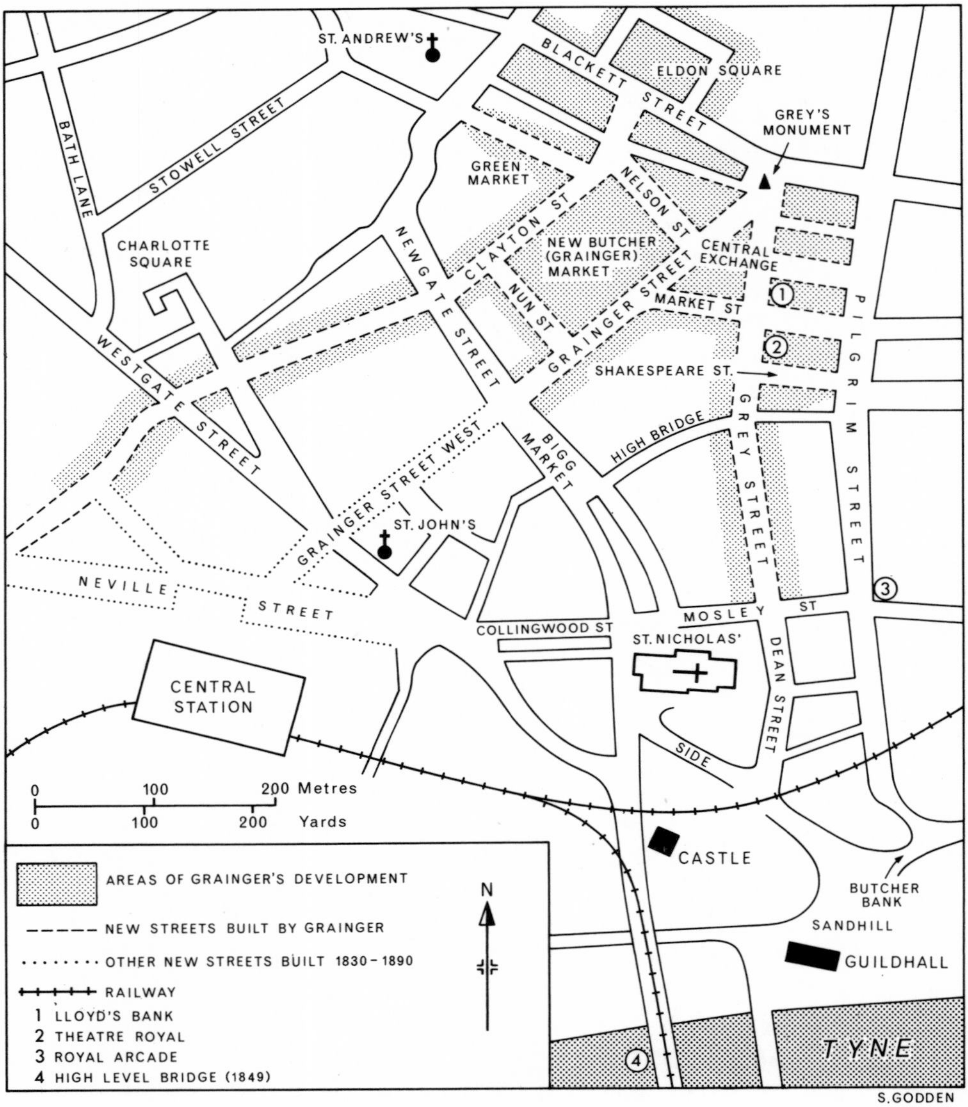
ST. ANDREW'S
BLACKETT STREET
ELDON SQUARE
GREY'S MONUMENT
BATH LANE
STOWELL STREET
GREEN MARKET
NELSON ST
CLAYTON ST
NEW BUTCHER (GRAINGER) MARKET
CENTRAL EXCHANGE
CHARLOTTE SQUARE
NEWGATE STREET
NUN ST
GRAINGER STREET
MARKET ST
PILGRIM STREET
WESTGATE STREET
SHAKESPEARE ST.
HIGH BRIDGE
GREY STREET
BIGG MARKET
GRAINGER STREET WEST
ST. JOHN'S
NEVILLE STREET
COLLINGWOOD ST
MOSLEY ST
ST. NICHOLAS'
DEAN STREET
CENTRAL STATION
SIDE
0 100 200 Metres
0 100 200 Yards
CASTLE
BUTCHER BANK
SANDHILL
GUILDHALL
TYNE
N
AREAS OF GRAINGER'S DEVELOPMENT
NEW STREETS BUILT BY GRAINGER
OTHER NEW STREETS BUILT 1830 - 1890
RAILWAY
1 LLOYD'S BANK
2 THEATRE ROYAL
3 ROYAL ARCADE
4 HIGH LEVEL BRIDGE (1849)
S.GODDEN

12. The Newcastle of Grainger and Dobson

forward on 22 May 1834, and on 12 July the council voted for the scheme by 24 to seven.

Grainger's plan was for shopping and commercial development based on three new main streets. The upper Lort Burn was to be filled in, and Upper Dean Street built over it from Mosley Street up to Blackett Street. A second street (Grainger Street) was to run from this junction on Blackett Street to the Bigg Market. The third street (Clayton Street) was to be built from further west on Blackett Street to Newgate Street, and beyond to Westgate, the last section 'to be built by a Joint Stock Company'. Extending Dean Street northwards meant knocking down the Theatre Royal in Mosley Street and the Flesh or Butcher Market (only established in 1808) which lay behind it, and Grainger had to agree to replace these.

The speed of execution of the plan almost equalled that of its acceptance. Grainger had already arranged the land purchase with Anderson's executors. He paid £50,000 for this and £45,000 for other necessary property. By 6 August the *Newcastle Journal* reported that earth from the Nun's Field was being moved to fill the Lord Burn. Two hundred and fifty thousand cartloads (at 2d. [0.8p] a load) were shifted. By October 1835 the new Flesh Market (now the Grainger Market), containing an incredible 180 butchers' shops, was finished, as well as the fruit and vegetable market on the other side of Clayton Street. The rest of the scheme was completed by 1839. It employed as many as 2,000 men at one time, and produced not only nine streets, but also 10 inns, 12 public houses, 325 shops with homes attached, and 40 private houses, as well as the major buildings like the Theatre Royal in Upper Dean Street, and the magnificent Central Exchange. The semi-circular interior of this Exchange became a newspaper room, with 'a spacious promenade' around it. 'It is', writes an 1855 pamphleteer, 'in the leisure hours of evening, in the Central Exchange . . . that the mind relaxes and is relieved from the fag of business, from the tension and anxiety of commercial enterprise'.

The finest achievement was not an individual building, but the total rising sweep of Upper Dean Street (Plate 32), re-named Grey Street in 1836 in honour of Earl Grey of the Reform Bill. At the summit Grey's Monument was erected in 1838 as a focus for the entire scheme. Throughout his property development Grainger built to a high standard, and used quality materials, facing his buildings with stone from local quarries at Kenton and Elswick rather than with the painted stucco surfaces commonly used. The buildings had sewers and water-closets, and Grainger had the street lit with gas and the road surfaces macadamised. The total scheme cost some £646,000, and Grainger later told the 1854 Cholera Commissioners that he had decorated the

Corner of Central Exchange

Theatre Royal portico

frontages of his buildings 'because it pleased him to do it, though the cost had probably been not less than £100,000'.

Grainger employed a number of architects on his various schemes. Thomas Oliver designed Blackett Street and the Leazes development, and John and Benjamin Green designed the new Theatre Royal and surrounding buildings. Most notable was John Dobson, already the main northern architect in the 1820s. As well as his many country houses, Dobson remodelled the Guildhall in 1823–6 and designed St. Thomas's church and St. Mary's Place. For Grainger he designed Eldon Square, and in the 1830s plan he did the new markets and the east side of Grey Street from Mosley Street up to Shakespeare Street. Dobson has often been credited with much more of the scheme, but a great deal was done by two architects in Grainger's office, John Wardle and George Walker.

Although Grainger was a wealthy man by 1834, he could not finance this massive property development from his own funds. The construction was financed by mortgages on the security of existing buildings. Each new block completed meant another mortgage to pay off existing debts and finance further development. From 1835 to 1838 Grainger raised £102,457 on successive mortgages. Clayton himself advanced £7,500, and doubtless helped persuade other leading citizens and banks. Robert Allgood put in £9,000, Matthew Clayton £7,100, and Messrs. Backhouse and Co., the bankers, £11,750. Grainger was very reluctant to sell property and hoped to repay out of rents, but this was a lengthy process and Grainger really depended, like many a modern developer, on the building boom continuing. So by 1839 he was looking for another property coup.

He was also disillusioned by opposition to some of his ideas. As with the Royal Arcade in 1832, so his Central Exchange was rejected as a new corn exchange by the corporation, despite his offer of it 'at such price as they thought reasonable and (he) would not require payment until the tolls of the market produced the money'. His plans in 1838 for a new Guildhall and Courts at the top of Grey Street were also rejected, and he built the Northumberland and Durham District Bank (now Lloyds Bank) instead. These and other setbacks (like the stopping of Grainger Street's extension to the new Neville Street) encouraged Grainger to look for a new site where he would have a freer hand.

On 2 January 1839 Grainger purchased the Elswick estate west of the town from John Hodgson Hinde for £114,100. Grainger saw the area as the potential terminus for the new railway system, with factories and residential terraces in the vicinity. However, he already had large debts, and the new £103,942 in mortgages to purchase

Elswick led to his security toppling in 1841 and his creditors demanding payment. He only avoided bankruptcy through Clayton's efforts, and the creditors were persuaded to accept gradual repayment. Grainger was forced to live modestly, parts of Elswick were sold off, notably the riverside site to Armstrong for an engineering works in 1847, and the rest gradually built up as the Elswick factories grew. At Grainger's death in 1861 his debts still totalled £128,582, but by 1901 the Elswick estates had been sold to pay them all off, and the rest of the estate was worth over £1,000,000. Dobson died in 1865 leaving a comfortable £16,000, but the cautious and shrewd Clayton left £729,000 at his death in 1890.

John Dobson

In Grainger's plan Grey Street and Dean Street were to be the main commercial thoroughfare of the town, but this did not last more than 10 years. The coming of the railway in 1849 and the building of Dobson's Central Station in Neville Street and the High Level Bridge for both rail and road traffic at the head of the Side, shifted attention from Grainger's axis. By the 1880s the old-fashioned shops of Grey Street with their houses above them were losing prestige to the new shops in Northumberland Street and Grainger Street West (opened 1868), and the shopkeepers petitioned for a rent reduction. Ironically, this very decline has undoubtedly preserved facades that would have been destroyed if Grey Street had remained the main thoroughfare.

The narrow lanes and slums of Sandgate and the Quayside were left out of this central area development. If anything, conditions became worse and more overcrowded during this period, one of rapid population growth and later Irish immigration. Typhus was endemic in these areas, which were also first and hardest hit in any outbreak, such as cholera in 1831, the scarlatina epidemic of 1845–47, and the so-called 'Irish fever' of 1846–48. A survey by Dr. D. B. Reid in 1845 found 33 streets near the Quayside without either drains or sewers, and running water was only available in the better parts of the town. In 1853 the cholera epidemic took 1,533 lives, a mortality rate of only one in 189 in rural Jesmond, but one in 43 in St. Nicholas's parish. In October 1854 there was a great fire in Gateshead, which an explosion spread to Newcastle, and the west end of the Quayside and the lanes behind were all burnt out, to be replaced by King, Queen, and Lombard Streets, and new commercial buildings. However, it was not until late in the century that the other slums of riverside Newcastle were pulled down for commercial development and the working population found improved housing in the terraced streets of Scotswood, Elswick and east Byker.

XXIII Government and Reform, 1800-1850

In 1800 Northumberland was represented in Parliament by two members, usually from leading county families, elected by a very restricted franchise. Newcastle also had two M.P.s elected by the burgesses (freemen), but in practice they were members of the oligarchy. Morpeth also had two M.P.s, who were nominees of the Howards, Earls of Carlisle. Party labels of Whig and Tory often meant little until election time, and then there was frequently no contest and the seats were split. The 1826 election showed the costs of a contest: in the Northumberland county constituency nearly £250,000 was spent, and T. W. Beaumont of the lead family was said to have spent £11,000 in the public houses of Alnwick Ward alone. Two politicians, J. G. Lambton (later first Lord Durham) and T. W. Beaumont, fought a duel on Bamburgh sands after heated words at Alnwick. Law and order in the county was controlled by the magistrates, headed by the Lord Lieutenant, the Duke of Northumberland, and responsible to the Home Secretary in London. Newcastle was a separate entity with its mayor and magistrates, who also controlled the river Tyne down to its mouth.

This political structure gave little voice to the middle-class and professional groups who were becoming more significant, and none at all to the working man, and after 1815 a reform movement grew, aided by the economic recession of the post-war years. On Tyneside radical societies of Political Protestants were formed and the *Tyne Mercury* expressed radical opinion. Although there was much popular support, the leaders were middle-class, with varied ideas on reform. James Losh, barrister and Tyneside industrialist, was for limited franchise reform, but against the secret ballot, and others of similar outlook included Dr. Headlam the wealthy physician, Turner the Unitarian minister, and Charnley the bookseller. More reformist was John Fife, a dynamic young surgeon and founder of the Newcastle Eye Infirmary, and on the radical wing, advocating the vote for all men and the secret ballot, were Thomas Doubleday, soap-maker and political economist (now perhaps best remembered for his *Coquetdale Fishing Songs*), Charles Attwood the industrialist, and the publisher W. A. Mitchell.

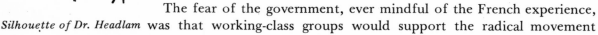

Silhouette of Dr. Headlam

The fear of the government, ever mindful of the French experience, was that working-class groups would support the radical movement with force. On Tyneside the main working groups with economic bargaining power were the pitmen, the keelmen and the seamen working the colliers, and there was a long history of disputes over wages and conditions of work. There was a major coal strike in 1765 over the annual bond or contract, seamen's strikes in the 1790s and in 1815, and numerous keelmen's strikes over overloading and the employment threat of the new spouts, notably in 1809, 1819, and 1822. There was, in fact, little connection between political activity and these industrial disputes. There were, of course, supporters of radicalism, but there was no organised connection, and for the most part, as Professor N. McCord has said, 'far from acting for the transformation of existing society, their eyes were fixed on more immediate and more practical concerns'. Government figures like the Newcastle mayor and the Lords Lieutenant usually recognised this, though alarmist magistrates bombarded the Home Secretary with warnings. Extra troops and a naval presence on the Tyne were normally requested during disputes, but the authorities did not simply side with employers and repress strikers. Rather they tried to mediate. Their sympathy was, of course, strictly limited: they tolerated no interference with property, were inclined to prosecute strike-leaders after some disputes, and were willing to use force if no agreement could be reached, as in the 1815 seamen's strike.

Grey's Monument, Newcastle

The crisis year of 1819 illustrates these relationships. On 16 August 11 people were killed by troops and many injured in a radical demonstration in Manchester, which became known as the 'Peterloo massacre'. There was widespread protest, and in Newcastle the local radicals planned a big meeting on the Town Moor for 11 October. This unrest coincided with the keelmen's strike, and 300 ships were idle on the Tyne. The Newcastle mayor, Archibald Reed, called for extra troops and ships, but the mass meeting, chaired by Eneas MacKenzie the bookseller and publisher, went off peacefully, even though Reed estimated 40,000 were there in total. The strike was virtually ignored by all radical speeches. Even the Tory *Newcastle Courant* thought it had no political content, whilst the *Mercury* was actually against strikes as restraints on free trade. Reed came under pressure from coal-owners, and so on 14 October he sailed on the steam-packet *Speedwell* to North Shields with some naval boats, escorting some blackleg keels. When he was in the *Northumberland Arms* on the New Quay at Shields, a crowd stoned the keels and packet. Two marines fired and killed a man. The crowd erupted and attacked the inn, and Reed had to escape by the back door. That evening dragoons from Newcastle cleared the streets, but the authorities still tried for a negotiated settlement and the strike ended on 22 October. In December, however, the

Northumberland and Newcastle Volunteer Cavalry were formed 'for local protection of property and in aid of the civil power'.

With economic improvement and slightly more liberal policies after 1820, popular support for reform declined until the end of the decade, when the Whig government of Earl Grey, himself a Northumbrian, came into office pledged to moderate reform, and was vehemently opposed by Wellington and most Tories. In Newcastle there were many public meetings to press for reform and an uneasy alliance of Whigs, liberals and Radicals was formed in the Northern Political Union in June 1831, with Losh, Headlam, Fife, Doubleday, and Attwood, but not conservative Whigs like Sir Matthew Ridley. Feelings ran high, and the tension was increased by a bitter miners' strike that year, and the bitter reaction of employers the next. Opponents of reform like the Duke of Northumberland and Lord Londonderry were vilified, and there was great rejoicing when the Reform Bill was finally passed in 1832. Grey became a hero in the north. The Bill gave the vote to £10 householders in boroughs, and to most farmers in the counties. The constituencies were re-drawn: Northumberland was split into north and south constituencies, each with two members. Newcastle continued with two members, but Morpeth was reduced to one, and a new constituency was created at Tynemouth (as at Gateshead and South Shields).

Many Whigs and moderate reformers had now achieved their Parliamentary goals, and as soon as the Reform Bill was passed, the uneasy alliance of the N.P.U. broke up. John Fife resigned within a week of the new Act. Some reformers now turned their attention to Newcastle's town government, where a running battle between the oligarchy and wider group of burgesses had been going on since 1829. The burgesses wanted a greater say, and there was a series of riotous guild meetings. In the Christmas 1831 guild meeting they protested against Grainger's corn market proposals and the 'interests of a private speculator' and implied Clayton had a corrupt interest, and the proposals were dropped. In 1832 the burgesses put up a rival mayoral candidate, but the manoeuvres of the oligarchy managed to defeat them. Fife, steward of the Barber-Surgeons' company, attacked the 'vile and corrupt' corporation and its new Peelite police as 'the mere tools of a political oligarchy, the instruments of tyranny, and the panderers of corruption'. Fife was given to extreme language, though there was some evidence of leading men like Robert Bell and Clayton getting advantageous leases of town property. Many reformers and Radicals did not join this campaign, however, since they did not think the burgesses a representative group. The resident freemen numbered 1,500 to 1,700, and after the Reform Bill 365 were £10 householders, compared with 2,811 non-freemen. At national level there were moves

John Clayton

for municipal reform and after a royal commission, the Municipal Corporations Act of 1835 brought in the household franchise to town government. The Whigs and reformers won town office that year, though Clayton remained as town clerk and symbol of the old system until 1867.

Thomas Doubleday

In the late 1830s Tyneside radicalism revived with the national Chartist movement for further Parliamentary reform based on the secret ballot and manhood suffrage. Doubleday revived the N.P.U. in 1838, and though the Chartist movement had wide working-class support, the main Tyneside leaders (apart from Hepburn, the pitmen's leader) were middle-class radicals, though there was no Whig or liberal support this time. Many meetings were held, addressed by national speakers like Feargus O'Connor. Through the winter into 1839 the Chartist voice became more strident, and especially after the Chartist Petition was rejected in July, there was talk of violence, and a general strike or 'Sacred Month' was called for August. Many Chartists were arming, and the North Shields magistrates' clerks reported later 'several pikes have been taken from the Chartists and 60 more have been given up voluntarily'. Troops were strengthened in Newcastle and 500 special constables sworn in. When John Fife (ironically the mayor this year) banned a meeting at the Forth ground on 30 July many still turned up, and clashed with the authorities in central Newcastle. Colonel Campbell told the crowd to disperse or 'his grenadiers would fire upon them', and Fordyce later wrote 'the cavalry galloped along the streets, up passages and lanes (around St. Nicholas's Square), the affrighted people rushing in all directions to find shelter'. The 'battle of the Forth' ended in 30 arrests, but not a single serious injury. The August strike (reduced to a few days) was a fiasco and only a few collieries came out. There was no readiness to use force to gain political change and Chartism on Tyneside rapidly declined.

The political reforms since 1800 were in some ways very modest. They gave the vote to the middle-classes and professions in the towns and to the tenant farmers in the county, but nothing to the wage-earners and farm workers. In the county constituencies the same landed families became M.P.s—the Ridleys, Beaumonts, Percies, Liddells, Greys, and Lambtons. Many elections remained uncontested, and Morpeth's single seat remained in Howard control and saw no election from the Reform Bill until 1874.

The new House of Commons did, however, give some political power to the manufacturers and industrialists who already controlled considerable economic power (the new Tynemouth constituency, for example, was largely created to represent the shipping interest), and if there had been no 1832 Bill, men like Fife and Headlam may have been on the side of revolt in 1839. The limited reforms opened up the road to gradual extension of the franchise, and the most remarkable achievement of these years that saw tremendous economic and social change (very visible on Tyneside) was that society managed to avoid polarisation and absorbed change with so little conflict or bloodshed.

The New Quay and Northumberland Arms, North Shields

XXIV The Victorian Economy

Pitman c.1900

The Victorian era brought dramatic changes in the economy of the North-east. There was unprecedented industrialisation and population expansion, with new villages and towns springing up in the south-east of Northumberland. Yet the Victorian period could have been one of stagnation and decline on Tyneside, for although the wind seemed set fair in the 1840s, much of Tyneside's existing industry was to decline in the following decades, and only the energies of Tyneside entrepreneurs put the region on a new direction of growth.

The major exception to this decline was coalmining itself. After 1850, with the expansion of local railways and the growing demand for steam-coal, the pace of growth quickened. Mining around Seghill, Plessey and Cramlington was extended. Districts previously mined for High Main coal were re-opened for steam-coal. Collieries became larger, and new settlements grew up, like East Hartford after 1866. Coal was taken by rail to the Tyne, where the Northumberland Dock opened in 1857. These railways (and the advent of steamships) made the small harbour of Seaton Sluice redundant. Collieries north of Blyth were slower to expand because of transport problems, for Blyth was a private port for Cowpen colliery. Netherton colliery, opened in the 1820s, shipped its coal via keels on Sleekburn gut (channel) until, with Bedlington and Barrington pits, it gained rail access to the Tyne in 1850. In 1854 Blyth harbour was opened up and improved, but could not cope with the volume: by 1860 it was shipping 250,000 tons, whereas 1½ million tons went by Blyth-Tyne railway. New mining villages, like Bomarsund, named after an engagement in the Crimean War, sprang up north of the river Blyth. In 1872 the railway was extended to Ashington. Coal from here and neighbouring collieries like Pegswood and Newbiggin had a long rail journey to the Northumberland Dock, and in 1882 the Blyth Harbour Commissioners began major improvements at Blyth. Blyth shipped only 150,000 tons in 1883, but 4,750,000 tons in 1913. Ashington's population grew from 1,002 in 1871, to 5,307 in 1891, 13,972 in 1901, and nearly 25,000 in 1911. Beyond Ashington, pits around Amble were extended for the deep steam-coal, creating new villages at Radcliffe and Broomhill, and Amble harbour and staithes were improved in the 1870s.

Though coalmining thrived, other sectors faltered at mid-century. The collier trade itself was threatened by the quicker and more reliable delivery of coal to London by railway from other regions. The recently-grown iron industry faced competition from Teesside with its Cleveland ores. The remote furnaces of Redesdale soon went out of business. Bedlington closed in 1860, Wylam in 1865. Tyneside ironworks managers migrated to Teesside, and though the Walker works of Losh, Wilson and Bell survived with its imported ore, they too closed in 1891. Similarly the Tyneside alkali industry declined in the face of the new Solvay process and the attractions of Teesside. The glass industry largely disappeared through new competition, and in south-west Northumberland the leadmining costs rose as lead prices fell with new foreign supplies entering the market, and the mines were closed.

The state of the river Tyne was a major constraint on industrial growth. Although the Tyne was one of Britain's leading ports, it was possible in the 1840s to ford the river below Newcastle at low tide, and vessels commonly grounded on banks and shoals. At the mouth there were no piers, and gales drove ships onto the Black Midden rocks. In 1849 the average depth on the bar was only six feet. Newcastle corporation was responsible for the river, but made few improvements, much to the annoyance of Tynesiders. From 1809 to 1849 the corporation received £957,973 from river dues, etc., but spent only £397,719, the rest going on town expenditure. In 1850, however, the Tyne Improvement Commission took control of the river, and after J. P. Ure became Engineer in 1859, dredging began. In 1876 the opening of the Swing Bridge at Newcastle, and further dredging beyond it, opened up the river to Dunston Staithes. By 1895 there was 30 feet of water even at low tide well up river, and the two massive piers at the mouth were complete.

New direction for the Tyneside economy after 1850 was provided by men like Charles Mark Palmer and William Armstrong. Palmer, a young coalowner, decided to build a steam-propelled iron ship to meet the competition of railway-marketed coal. His *John Bowes* was launched in 1852 and immediately proved its value, delivering as much coal to London in a five-day return trip as a collier would in two months. Further iron ships from Palmer's Jarrow yard and other shipyards not only saved the seaborne coal trade, but began a major shipbuilding industry. Existing wooden shipbuilding, of colliers and East Indiamen, did not die immediately. In 1858, only seven out of 44 Tyne shipyards used iron, but by 1862 there were 10 (including C. W. Mitchell's Walker yard), employing over 4,000 men.

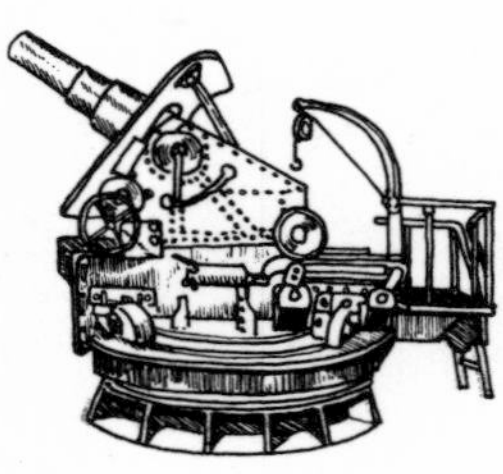

Armstrong gun

William Armstrong, an archetypal Victorian industrialist, made the biggest impact on Tyneside. The son of a corn merchant who was

Mayor of Newcastle, Armstrong began as a solicitor, but became more interested in engineering. He invented a hydraulic crane and started a small factory at Elswick in 1847. The Crimean War of 1854–6 provided opportunities for both Palmer and Armstrong. Palmer got a contract for a rolled-iron plated gunship, the *Terror,* 2,000 tons, with 16 300-pound guns, and later gained a reputation for warships. Armstrong invented a breech-loading field gun, soon adopted by the government. He was knighted, and Elswick became an armaments centre, which by the late 1860s was bigger than Palmer's yards.

H.M.S. Staunch

In 1867 Armstrong also began making warships, but as ships could not get up to Elswick, they were built at Mitchell's Walker yard, and the firms amalgamated in 1883. In 1876 Armstrong designed the hydraulic Swing Bridge, which enabled ships to reach Elswick riverfront, where a shipyard was opened in 1884. Armstrong's first warship was the gunboat *H.M.S. Staunch* in 1868, and he was soon building cruisers and gunboats for the world; the *Panther* for Austro-Hungary, the battleship *Victoria* for Britain, the *Elizabeta* for Rumania, the *Yashima* for Japan, and many others. The Armstrong empire also pioneered the steam-propelled tanker for the emerging oil trade, building the *Gluckauf* in 1886 as the first effective oil tank steamer, and 95 others in the next 20 years.

By 1900 Tyneside was a world famous centre for both shipbuilding and armaments. Armstrong's complex had grown from 30 men in 1847 to a workforce of over 25,000. The Tyne's reputation was not just based on the Armstrong and Palmer yards, but also on other major firms like Hawthorn, Leslie and Co., and Swan Hunter's. Marine engineering became important, with firms like Hawthorn's, Clarke Chapman of Gateshead, and Parsons' Heaton Works and his Marine Steam Turbine Company. C. A. Parsons developed the turbine engine, and his vessel *Turbinia* amazed the naval world at the 1897 Spithead review by weaving amongst the big warships at 30 knots. Parsons also developed turbo-alternators for electric power, and Tyneside firms became important suppliers to the new electricity industry. Although Tyneside's fame had not been built on passenger ships, Tynesiders have tended to see the crowning achievement of this era of growth as the large transatlantic liner *Mauretania,* built in 1906 by Swan Hunter's and powered by Parsons' turbines. The fastest transatlantic liner of her day, she continued the New York run until 1934.

This Victorian economic growth brought rapid population growth and in-migration. Wallsend, for example, grew from 4,700 in 1841 to 29,000 in 1901, and Elswick from 3,539 in 1851 to 27,801 in only 20 years. In 1871 a fifth of Northumberland's population had been born outside Northumberland and Durham. Thirty-one per cent. of these migrants had come from Scotland, and 19 per cent. were Irish. The different groups and the overcrowded housing led to tensions. When the anti-Catholic lecturer Murphy visited North Shields in 1869, there were shots in the hall and a major street-fight outside. Although great inequalities and considerable poverty remained, the economic growth brought higher living standards to the mass of the population, especially towards the end of the century. In particular, housing improved, together with sanitation and public health, and the new terraced streets of Scotswood, Byker and Wallsend represented very real advances on earlier conditions. For the middle-classes there were the larger terraces of Jesmond. The new housing greatly expanded Newcastle and the Tyneside towns, and the railways, horse-trams (introduced to Newcastle in 1879), and later electric trains and trams, helped men get to their work. The Tyneside landscape altered dramatically. In the 1840s watercolours and lithographs still showed grassy banks to the river, but by 1914 the river was largely flanked by terraced streets and shipyards.

The coast and sea-bathing had long attracted middle-class visitors. Assembly Rooms had been built at Tynemouth, and in 1843 the steamboat *Venus* had begun regular sailings from the New Quay, North Shields, to Seaton Sluice, providing a return ticket, plus tea and a plate of fruit at Seaton Delaval gardens, all for 1s. 3d. (6p). Now the shipyard managers and skilled workmen began to live in the Victorian and Edwardian terraces in Tynemouth, Cullercoats and Whitley, and many other workers made Sunday trips to the seaside there.

With rising living standards, some industrial disputes began to focus on working hours as well as wages. Industrialists like Armstrong were generous in gifts to Newcastle and other towns, but could be dictatorial in their factories. In 1871 Armstrong strongly opposed his engineers on strike for a nine-hour day, and brought in foreign blacklegs, but he eventually had to give way. This 1871 strike was not union-organised, and apart from the miners (who built an effective union in the 1860s), organised unionism only expanded in the 20 years before 1914.

Along with industrial growth on Tyneside came rural decline in Northumberland. Although farming wages were good compared with southern England, labourers left the farms for the towns of Tyneside and further afield. The population of the Ford district of Glendale fell by 43 per cent. in 1851-1901. Cheap railway transport allowed goods from industrial districts to drive rural industries out of production. Woollen mills, smithies, market town industries like glove-making at Hexham, all declined. As people left, a negative multiplier effect led to a downward spiral of rural services and amenities, a spiral still not halted in parts of Northumberland.

St. George's church, Cullercoats

31. Newcastle and the Tyne in 1825. On the river is one of the new steam boats.

32. Grey Street, Newcastle, in Victorian times.

33. Newcastle and the Tyne bridges in the late 1960s. New office blocks now dominate the view.

34. Guyzance Mill on the Coquet, together with the weir across to Whirleyshaws mentioned in a charter of 1356.

XXV Northumberland and Newcastle since 1914

The First World War took the lives of thousands of Northumbrians serving in France with the Northumberland Fusiliers and other regiments. It also brought extra orders to the Tyneside shipyards, and Armstrong's annual profits rose from £800,000 to £1 million. However, the end of the war also ended the era of world-wide imperial and trade expansion, and the boom ended in the summer of 1920, when freight rates suddenly fell and contracts for new ships dried up. The trade recession was accentuated by the lack of government naval orders, restricted by the Washington Naval Limitation Treaty and later by disarmament policies. By 1923 there was heavy unemployment on Tyneside, though there was a limited recovery, particularly with orders for oil tankers, after 1926. Armstrongs epitomised the problem: they built only one Admiralty warship between 1920 and 1936, and they desperately tried new projects like the disastrous Newfoundland paper-mills scheme, where costs escalated in a bad winter, and in 1927 they were forced to merge with Vickers. The Walker Naval Yard closed in 1928.

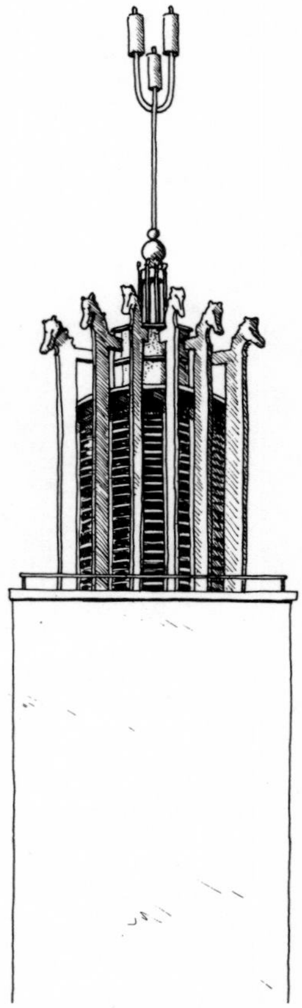

Bell-tower, Civic Centre, Newcastle

These were just the beginnings of bad times. In recessions long-term investment like shipbuilding is first and hardest hit, and the industry now suffered even more in the 1930s Depression. In 1930 orders for tankers ceased, yards began to close, and unemployment soared. Economic rock-bottom was in late summer 1932. At Willington unemployment was 74.6 per cent., in Wallsend 46 per cent., and in North Shields 48 per cent. The National Shipbuilders Security Company was set up in 1930 to buy redundant shipyards for other uses, and in 1934 Palmer's Jarrow yard on south Tyneside was bought and closed. All the related engineering industries also suffered, as did coalmining. Falling coal prices and exports in the post-1918 years had led to clashes between employers and miners over wages, culminating in the General Strike of 1926, and its sad failure to help the miners. Unemployment in Ashington reached 63 per cent. in summer 1932, and 55 per cent. in Bedlington, though these were seasonal peaks, and by winter the rates were down to 19 per cent. and 10.6 per cent. respectively.

Government cuts reinforced the downward spiral, and it was not until 1934 that positive action was taken. The particular problem of the region was its over-emphasis on a few basic industries and a failure to develop the newer growth industries like car and aircraft production. The commercial flexibility that led to new directions in the 1840s was not present in early 20th century Tyneside. Many people migrated to jobs in the Midlands and South-east. In 1934 the Special Areas Act set up development areas and finance to build industrial estates for new industry, but by 1934 the world economy was recovering, and with it shipping orders. On Tyneside rearmament gave a real injection: in 1935 the Walker Naval Yard re-opened and built the battleship *King George V,* and by September 1936 there were 17 warships under contract in Tyneside yards. Even in 1939, however, there was still high unemployment in many parts of the North-east. The 1930s recession (like that of the mid-1970s) was very uneven in its impact, and at the same time as the Jarrow workers were marching to London in 1936, there were many new estates of suburban semi-detached houses being built around Tyneside.

After the Second World War the North-east shared in the national rise in prosperity. Throughout the 1950s incomes rose, suburban estates expanded, and car ownership became more common. Output from the Northumberland coalfield expanded, and the Tyneside shipyards had full order books, especially for oil tankers, though there were also passenger ships like the *Empress of England* launched at Walker Naval Yard in 1956. However, the region's growth lagged behind the national rate: the area was still dependent on a few traditional industries, lacked rapid growth industries, and people continued to migrate to the faster-growing Midlands and South-east.

These underlying problems came to the surface after 1960. Shipbuilding was facing stiffer competition from Japan and Germany, and profits fell. The Blyth yard, with 1,000 employees, closed in 1966. The 1966 Geddes Report on British Shipbuilding argued for rationalisation, and in 1968 Swan Hunters merged with all the other Tyne yards to form Swan, Hunter and Tyne Shipbuilders, but the future has remained uncertain, and in 1976 the industry faces nationalisation. Coalmining also contracted; the number of miners in the whole North-east fell from 140,000 in 1958 to 63,000 in 1969. In Northumberland, towns like Amble, Ashington and Bedlington saw increasing mining unemployment, although a number of pits in the area were designated as long-life pits by the N.C.B.

This decline, and the fact that regions like Tyneside were always first to go under in a recession like that of 1962–63 and last to recover, made the government step up its regional policies and incentives to new industries, aided by local organisations like the North East Development Council. Attracting these industries has been difficult. The region has had an unfavourable image, and is seen

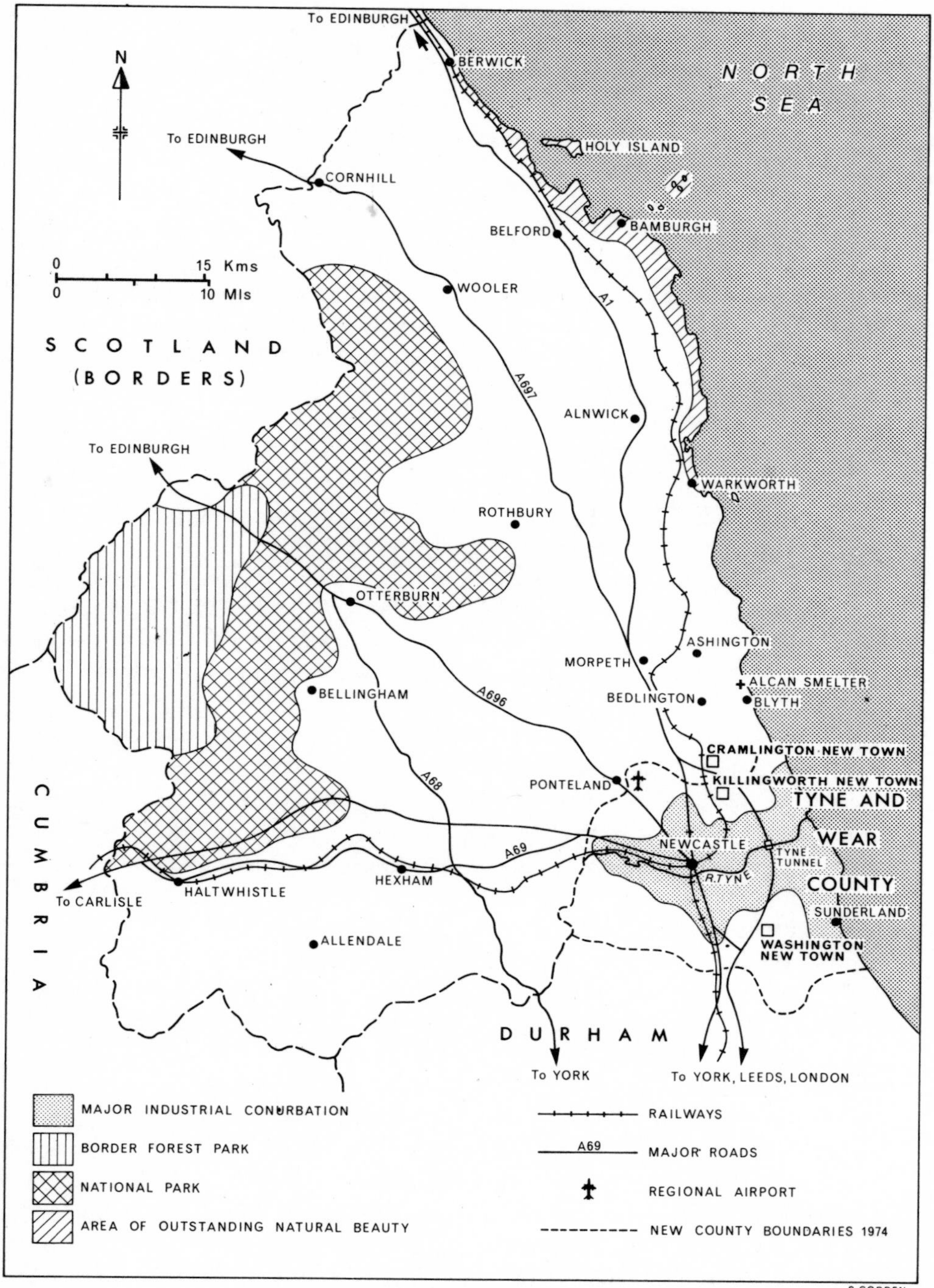

To EDINBURGH
BERWICK
NORTH SEA
N
To EDINBURGH
HOLY ISLAND
CORNHILL
BELFORD
BAMBURGH
0 15 Kms
0 10 Mls
WOOLER
A1
SCOTLAND
(BORDERS)
A697
ALNWICK
To EDINBURGH
WARKWORTH
ROTHBURY
OTTERBURN
ASHINGTON
MORPETH
ALCAN SMELTER
BELLINGHAM
A696
BEDLINGTON
BLYTH
CRAMLINGTON NEW TOWN
A68
PONTELAND
KILLINGWORTH NEW TOWN
CUMBRIA
TYNE AND WEAR COUNTY
NEWCASTLE
A69
TYNE TUNNEL
HEXHAM
R.TYNE
To CARLISLE
HALTWHISTLE
SUNDERLAND
ALLENDALE
WASHINGTON NEW TOWN
DURHAM
To YORK
To YORK, LEEDS, LONDON
MAJOR INDUSTRIAL CONURBATION
BORDER FOREST PARK
NATIONAL PARK
AREA OF OUTSTANDING NATURAL BEAUTY
RAILWAYS
A69 MAJOR ROADS
REGIONAL AIRPORT
NEW COUNTY BOUNDARIES 1974
S.GODDEN

13. Northumberland and Tyneside in 1976

Swan House, Pilgrim Street, Newcastle

as remote from the centres of the Midlands and South-east, where the potential migrant firms are, though the new road system based on the Tyne Tunnel and A1(M) is a major improvement. The new industries have also tended to employ the reserves of female labour rather than the unemployed men, and to require modern skills difficult to find in the area. In face of these difficulties the success of the policy has been remarkable. Numerous firms have come, and the regional economy would be in a much worse state today without them. In 1968 the government directed the new Alcan aluminium smelter, costing £50 million, to Lynemouth, ensuring the jobs of perhaps 1,000 miners in the local pits. Despite all this, however, industrial Northumberland and Tyneside has again been hard hit by the mid-1970s recession. In June 1976 Tyneside unemployment stood at 8.2 per cent., against a national rate of 5.6 per cent., and it will be one of the slower regions to partake in any recovery of the British economy.

During the 1960s Northumberland County Council began two new towns at Killingworth (1962) and Cramlington (1963) to provide centres for new industry and housing in south-east Northumberland, and they have grown rapidly. In Newcastle the city planning officer, Dr. Wilfred Burns, and the leader of the City Council, Mr. T. Dan Smith, inaugurated a massive city centre redevelopment plan, involving a new road system (including an urban motorway) to relieve traffic congestion, and office and shopping complexes. Mr. Smith talked of creating 'the Brasilia of the Old World'. Older housing in Byker and Scotswood was pulled down, to be replaced with high-rise flats. The plan is not yet complete (and parts have been changed), but the city horizon is now dominated by new office blocks (Plate 33), the road system is much improved (though it has destroyed the human scale of parts of the city), and an underground railway or 'Metro' is still under construction. The central scheme has cost the city some of its fine buildings (notably Eldon Square), though it is perhaps the philosophy of huge housing blocks (like the 'Byker Wall' block shielding the rest of the neighbourhood from the motorway) that is most open to criticism.

The growing urban sprawl of Tyneside and the increase in commuting meant the existing local government units no longer represented defined communities. Many of Newcastle's suburbs lay in Northumberland county. In 1974 the national reorganisation of local government created a new Metropolitan County of Tyne and Wear to run the whole conurbation as one unit. Its boundaries included Newcastle, Tynemouth, and the Tyneside portions of Northumberland such as Gosforth, Wallsend and Whitley Bay. The new Northumberland administrative county was not reduced to a purely rural unit, as some earlier proposals had suggested, but retained much of the coalfield area, including Ashington, Blyth and Cramlington.

In the Northumberland countryside, population decline has continued as a result of farming mechanisation and the lack of job opportunities. Between 1956 and 1966 the agricultural labour force fell by almost 30 per cent. The problem has been most acute in Northumbrian Tweedside, where the population fell by 12.5 per cent. in 1951-61. Glendale fell by 7.2 per cent., and Haltwhistle by 8.2 per cent. Many small settlements have fallen below the viable size for community life. In Redesdale and North Tynedale the plantations of the Forestry Commission, started in the late 1920s, but greatly expanded since 1945, have provided some employment. Surveys of rural migration throughout the county have shown that lack of jobs for the young is a key factor, and it is the school-leavers who have to seek training and employment on Tyneside. Rural policy has evolved more slowly than industrial policy, but since the early 1960s planning documents have begun to emphasise the importance of rural growth centres, notably Morpeth, Hexham and Berwick, with secondary centres at Alnwick, Wooler and Haltwhistle.

With rising car ownership, the urban population of Tyneside has made increasing use of the Northumbrian countryside. The recent road improvements in industrial Northumberland, and the by-passes at Alnwick and Morpeth have also made the moors, hills and beaches more accessible. Public access to these areas is vital, but requires planning to avoid damaging both the environment and agriculture. To meet this need the Northumberland National Park was created in 1956, with its Warden centre at Ingram, whilst an Area of Outstanding Natural Beauty was designated on the coast between Warkworth and Berwick in 1958. Although the Northumberland countryside is uncongested compared with Devon or the Lake District, and one can still find half-empty beaches in north Northumberland in summer, specific areas have come under heavy pressure. The dune ecosystems of the coast are particularly fragile, and uncontrolled parking and development could lead to irreversible changes, so planning policy has restricted parking development to limited sites.

The historical legacy is also threatened. Parts of Hadrian's Wall are in danger from the thousands of tourists' feet. But the major threat is not to the older buildings and monuments (many of which are protected), but to the industrial and mining remains, being destroyed by modern urban and industrial change. Fortunately some of the best examples of industrial archaeology have been preserved, and can now be seen in the regional open-air industrial museum at Beamish in County Durham.

St. Mary's Island, Whitley Bay

XXVI Guyzance: A Local Landscape

Chancel remains, Brainshaugh nunnery

The history of a county cannot be neatly summarised in a concluding chapter. What one can do is illustrate the intertwining of some of the themes in that history by looking at one small area, a landscape in miniature. Almost any locality in the county could be chosen, but one such landscape can be found on the Coquet a few miles east of Felton. A turning off the A1 north of Felton leads down to a winding, wooded stretch of the river. The lands around this spot, north and south of the Coquet, constitute the modern parish of Acklington, but this was only created in 1859, and previously they were the townships of Acklington and Acklington Park and the chapelry of Guyzance or Brainshaugh.

The first record of this landscape is found in Symeon's *History of the Church at Durham,* where he documents that in 737 Ceolwulf, the Northumbrian king, retired to become a monk at Lindisfarne, giving estates at Warkworth and Bregesne (Brainshaugh) to the Church. Acklington, farm of the sons of Aeccel, is a fairly early Anglian settlement, sited on an outcrop above the clay. Guyzance, named after Guines, near Calais, is one of the few Norman place-names in the county. In Norman Northumberland the two sides of the Coquet were in different baronies: Guyzance was part of the knight's fee the Tisons held from the de Vescis of Alnwick, and Acklington was part of the Clavering barony at Warkworth. In the early medieval period the Coquet formed a significant legal boundary: the county had two coroners, one for 'citra Coquet', south of the river, and one 'ultra Coquet', based at Bamburgh. Richard Tison in or before 1147 founded a nunnery at Brainshaugh and gave this to the canons of Alnwick, together with some ploughland 'et cum halghe, ubi est ecclesia', and with the haugh where the church is. The remains of this nunnery and its Norman architecture still stand in the haugh by the river (Plate 9). In 1306–7 Edward I confirmed the right of Guyzance nunnery to pasture their cattle on Edlingham moor.

Both Guyzance and Acklington had open-field agriculture. In 1248 the bondagers of Acklington each held 30 acres, but had to work three days a week on the demesne land that Roger Fitzjohn had in the village, and harvest the corn. On the north side of Guyzance the Cistercian monks at Sturton Grange grazed their sheep on the moor. In 1240 these monks came to a detailed agreement with Alexander

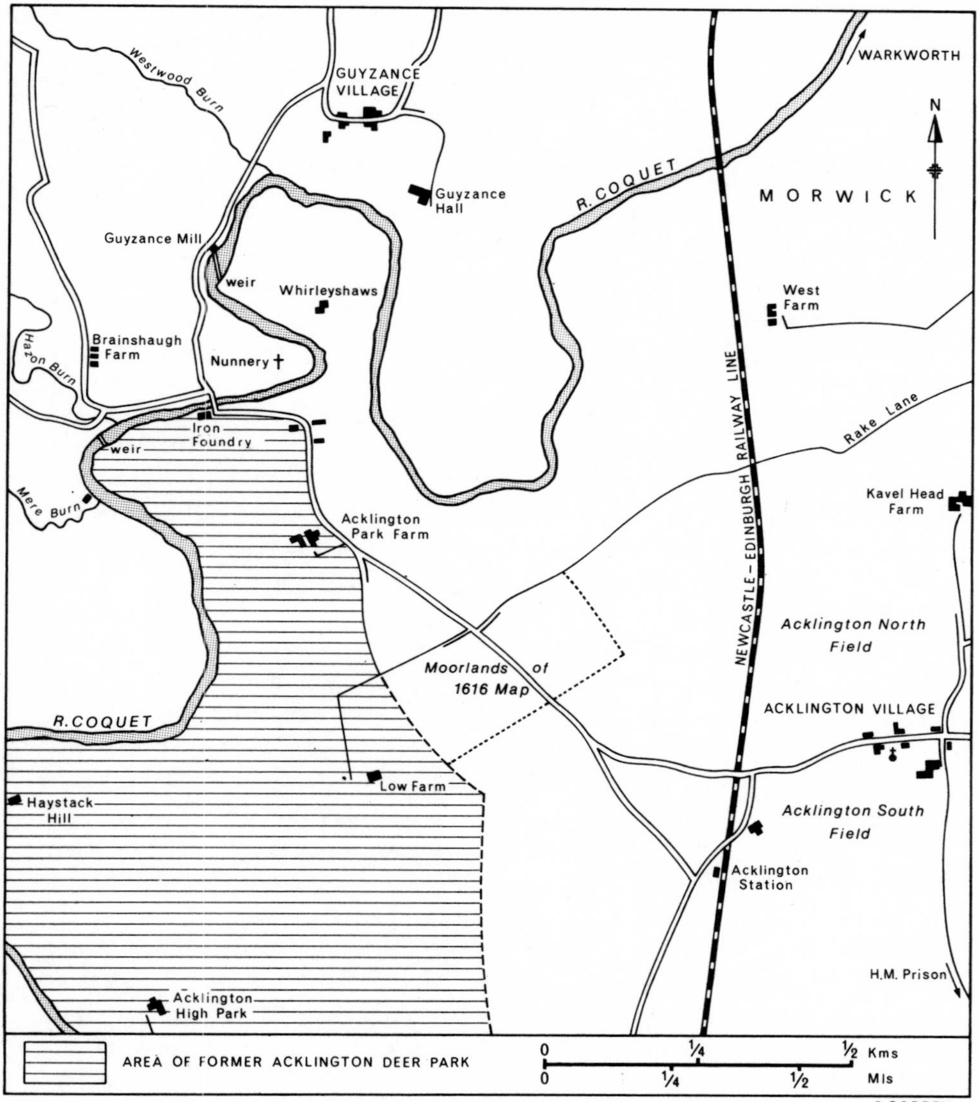
GUYZANCE VILLAGE
WARKWORTH
N
Westwood Burn
Guyzance Hall
R. COQUET
MORWICK
Guyzance Mill
weir
Whirleyshaws
West Farm
Brainshaugh Farm
Hazon Burn
Nunnery
NEWCASTLE – EDINBURGH RAILWAY LINE
Iron Foundry
weir
Rake Lane
Mere Burn
Kavel Head Farm
Acklington Park Farm
Acklington North Field
Moorlands of 1616 Map
R.COQUET
ACKLINGTON VILLAGE
Low Farm
Haystack Hill
Acklington South Field
Acklington Station
H.M. Prison
Acklington High Park
AREA OF FORMER ACKLINGTON DEER PARK
0 1/4 1/2 Kms
0 1/4 1/2 Mls
S.GODDEN

14. Guyzance and Acklington

Arms of Hilton

de Hilton about their boundaries with Guyzance and Shilbottle. The coal for the monks' forge came from Midilwood in Acton and was probably carted through Brainshaugh and Guyzance on its way.

Acklington, located on the plateau, had a windmill to grind corn, but Guyzance had a watermill on the Coquet. The 1336 subsidy roll lists Johannes molendinarius, John the miller, and in 1356 Sir Robert de Hilton obtained permission from Sir Henry Percy, who held Warkworth barony, to make a mill-race and weir across the river from the Guyzance bank to Whirleyshaws 'pro duccione aquae usque ad molendinum fullonicum', in order to lead water to the fulling mill (to make cloth). A later document records that each tenant had to repair eight feet of the mill dam for each husbandland he held. A successor to these mills still stands, disused, and the weir still runs across to Whirleyshaws (Plate 34).

The Scots' wars and Black Death affected the district. The latter may have destroyed the nunnery, and in 1352 at Acklington nine of the 35 bondage holdings were waste. Labour remained scarce, for in 1368 they were still waste, though used for pasture, and the 70 acres of demesne were rented out to tenants at 6d. (2½p) an acre. The Craster family, whom we have traced through these chapters, appear even here. In 1498 a Robert Crawcester was a tenant in Guyzance and a William in Acklington, and in 1540–1 William Crawster was the Guyzance bailiff.

The south bank of the river was set aside as a deer park by the lords of Warkworth. In 1248 it was described as a park with a perimeter of four leagues, stocked with 'seven score beasts, specifically young stags and fawns, but not buck is to be found there; and there are seven or eight hinds and one hart of two or three years of age'. The park gradually became pastureland and farms, but remained well wooded. In 1585 there were 2,000 oak trees and 300 ash valued at £783.

Sometime after 1313 the nunnery had become a curacy of Alnwick, but after 1539 the buildings and lands, like much other monastic property, passed from the King through a succession of Newcastle and London merchants. By this time both villages were in Percy hands and detailed surveys were taken in 1567 and 1616, mapping out the open-fields and commons. These surveys gave the boundaries of the townships and many of these can still be traced on the ground, particularly the western boundary against Acton from the Morke Hawghe by the Coquet up the Mere burn and a pathway to the 'hye Kyng's streat' or Great North Road. In Acklington a new area called Moore lands had been recently 'taken of the common, and converted to arable', and strips in this field had been allocated on a strict system: Henry Jackson was given the first, twenty-first and forty-first. The present road down from Acklington station runs through this land. 'Whirleyshaws', the survey said, 'enclosed on ye one syde with ye pale of the parke envyrouned on two partes with the water Cokett, ys the beste and moste commodiouse parte of the commone', but it was also eaten by the cattle from Guyzance and Brainshaugh, and the survey suggested that enclosure would be the ideal solution, but this could not be done because of 'a common waye over at the forde of Brainshaugh which cannot be barred'.

The Earl's surveyors recommended division of the lands in both villages, but this was not achieved until the late 1600s, though the increasingly commercial land management of the Elizabethan and Jacobean period can be seen in the Percy estates here. Acklington Park was let leasehold as one large pasture farm, and rents like that for Guyzance Mill were increased: in 1581 the mill raised £1 6s. 8d. (£1.33p) for the Earl, but by 1612 it was £5.

Agreement to enclose the village fields took place at Guyzance in the 1660s, probably under Percy pressure, and at Acklington early in the 18th century. This was followed by the later enclosure of the surrounding commons (such as Guyzance Lee to the west in 1760), and the building of farmhouses away from the villages at Bank House, Guyzance Lee and Kavel (Cavil) Head in the late 18th and early 19th centuries. In the period of agricultural improvement and the Napoleonic Wars much of the farming land was devoted to arable: the 1801 crops returns for Warkworth parish (which included Acklington) had 1,441 acres recorded for wheat and 1,923 for oats, though only relatively small acreages of the turnips, peas and beans that the Glendale farmers emphasised. Chimney-stacks for the steam-driven wheat-threshers can still be seen at Kavel Head and Chesters farms in Acklington. The land was heavier, more clayey, than areas further north, and the farms benefited from the tile-draining of the 1840s and 1850s: by 1860 the Earl's agents had drained 44 per cent. of the acreage of Acklington High Park. In 1861 54 per cent. of the farm was arable, but during the agricultural depression and after, the area became dominantly pastoral like so many parts of Northumberland. The local landscape is not one of large country houses, but at the end of the 19th century a substantial portion of Guyzance was bought by a leading Newcastle industrial entrepreneur and shipowner, J. D. Milburn (who had built Milburn House in the Side at Newcastle). During the Edwardian years he had one of the last country houses in the county built at Guyzance.

During all these changes to the local economy, the neighbourhood of Guyzance and Acklington was not cut off from wider political

Arms of Milburn

and economic events. The medieval Newcastle mayors and merchants, the Actons, came from Acton village on the west side of Guyzance. In 1569 George Horsley of Acklington Park was one of the foolish few who followed Percy in the Rising of the Northern earls, and John Rushworth, a later tenant of Acklington Park, was one of the clerks in the House of Commons in 1640 when Charles I tried to arrest the five members. Thomas Lisle of neighbouring Hazon joined his Catholic friend, William Ord of Sturton Grange, in the Jacobite rebellion of 1715, though Thomas's brothers stayed at home.

Industry has not radically affected this landscape. In 1715 the antiquary Warburton noted a colliery in Acklington village, but the major Victorian exploitation of the northern fringes of the coalfield took place just to the east of Acklingon, where the new mining villages of Broomhill and Radcliffe came into being after 1850. However, in 1775 a group of speculators had got a lease of land by the river in Acklington Park to build a tin and iron foundry and also to erect a dam or weir to provide power. These works can still be seen today, to the west of the bridge over the river, and the waterfall they constructed is a magnificent sight. The iron was marketed from the port at Amble, but the business did not flourish, because of distance from markets, and it was sold in 1791 with 45 years of the lease still to run. It was taken over by a Newcastle woollen merchant, John Reed, who early in 1796 was advertising in the *Newcastle Courant* for weavers. This mill was discontinued in 1884.

Bridge over Coquet at Acklington Park

The area lay to the east of the major turnpikes, but the railway sliced through Acklington in the 1840s creating a small agricultural market at the station. However, apart from the construction of an air force base (now a prison) on the south side of Acklington, the locality, and particularly the part near the river at Guyzance, has remained agricultural and unspoilt, and standing by 'the haugh where the church is' one is surrounded by elements of a landscape that is the result of over 1,200 years of Northumbrian history since it was part of an Anglian Royal estate.

Bibliography

This bibliography is a guide to further reading on the history of Northumberland and Newcastle Upon Tyne. It is not a list of the references used in the writing of this book, nor a list of purely specialist studies. I have included one or two rarer but very readable books, like *Sir Gilbert de Middleton* and *Memorials of North Tyndale,* that are available through the County Library. It may, however, be useful, before suggesting further reading, to give some of the major reference sources.

Seal of Society of Antiquaries of Newcastle

CHIEFLY FOR REFERENCE

A valuable guide to sources and records in the main libraries and record offices is *Northumberland History: a brief guide to records and aids in Newcastle Upon Tyne,* by H. A. Taylor (1963: Northumberland County Council). A fine guide to published material is the *Local Catalogue* (1932) of books and pamphlets in Newcastle City Library, supplemented by the card-index there.

The main work on Northumberland is *A History of Northumberland* in 15 volumes, published from 1893 to 1940 by the County History Committee, covering large areas of the county, parish by parish. This magnificent study omitted those areas covered earlier by the Rev. J. Hodgson in his *History of Northumberland* (three parts in seven volumes, 1820–1858), now being reprinted by Frank Graham, and J. Raine, *The History and Antiquities of North Durham* (1852). Alnwick was also omitted, but studied in G. Tate, *The History of the Borough, Castle and Barony of Alnwick* (two volumes, 1866–1869). For Newcastle the classic reference is J. Brand, *The History and Antiquities of the Town and County of the Town of Newcastle Upon Tyne* (two volumes, 1789).

The major journal for new research work is *Archaeologia Aeliana,* published by the Society of Antiquaries of Newcastle in five series since 1822, together with their *Proceedings* in five series from 1855 to 1956. Major records have been published in the volumes of the Surtees Society, the Records Series of the Newcastle Upon Tyne Records Committee, and recently by the Records Series of the Society of Antiquaries. Other journals that often carry articles of interest are *Northern History* (Leeds, 1966 onwards) and the *Transactions of the Architectural and Archaeological Society of Northumberland and Durham.* Recent archaeological discoveries are reported in the *Journal of Roman Studies, Britannia, Medieval Archaeology* and *Industrial Archaeology. Northern History* contains reviews of recent journal literature on the North, together with details of the most important accessions to archive offices each year.

The main archive collections are in the Newcastle City Archives and the Northumberland Record Office (at Melton Park, Gosforth), together with the Newcastle City Library, the Library of the Society of Antiquaries and the University Library. Good collections of local history books can be found in particular in Newcastle City Library, North Shields Public Library and the Northumberland County Library at Morpeth, and many are available on request through local library services. A useful introduction to the study of local history in the county is given by T. H. Rowland (1973), *Discovering Northumberland: A handbook of local history* (Newcastle: Frank Graham).

FURTHER READING

Allsopp, B. (1967): *Historic Architecture of Newcastle Upon Tyne* (Newcastle: Oriel Press).

Allsopp, B., and U. Clark (1969): *Historic Architecture of Northumberland* (Newcastle: Oriel Press).

Atkinson, F. (1968): *The Great Northern Coalfield 1700–1900* (London: University Tutorial Press).

Atkinson, F. (1974): *The Industrial Archaeology of the North East*. Two vols. (Newton Abbott: David and Charles).

Bailey, J., and G. Culley (1805): *General view of the Agriculture of Northumberland* etc. Reprinted, with introduction by D. J. Rowe, 1972. (Newcastle: Frank Graham).

Baker, A. R. H., and R. A. Butlin, eds. (1973): *Studies of Field Systems in the British Isles* (Cambridge: University Press).

Barrow, G. W. S. (1973): *The Kingdom of the Scots* (London: Edward Arnold).

Bates, C. J. (1895): *The History of Northumberland* (London: Elliot Stock).

Beckensall, S. (1974): *The Prehistoric Carved Rocks of Northumberland* (Newcastle: Frank Graham).

Bell, R. C. (1971): *Tyneside Pottery* (London: Studio Vista).

Birley, E. (1961): *Research on Hadrian's Wall* (Kendall: Titus Wilson).

Cadogan, P. (1975): *Early Radical Newcastle* (Consett: Sagittarius Press).

Charlton, E. (1871): *Memorials of North Tyndale and Its Four Surnames* (Newcastle).

Charlton, L. E. O., ed. (1949): *The Recollections of a Northumbrian Lady, 1815–1866* (London: Jonathan Cape).

Dixon, D. D. (1895): *Whittingham Vale* (Newcastle: Andrew Reid).

Dixon, D. D. (1903): *Upper Coquetdale.* Reprinted, 1974 (Newcastle: Frank Graham).

Dougan, D. J. (1968): *The History of North East Shipbuilding* (London: Allen and Unwin).

Fraser, C. M. (1957): *A History of Antony Bek* (Oxford: Clarendon Press).

Fraser, C. M., ed. (1968): *The Northumberland Lay Subsidy Roll of 1296* (Newcastle: Society of Antiquaries, Record Series, No. 1).

Fraser, C. M., and K. Emsley (1973): *Tyneside* (Newton Abbott: David and Charles).

Gard, R., ed. (1970): *Northumberland at the Turn of the Century* (Newcastle: Oriel Press).

Graham, F. (1974): *Northumbria's Lordly Strand* (Newcastle: Frank Graham).

Hall, M. (1973): *The Artists of Northumbria* (Newcastle: Marshall Hall Associates).

Honeyman, H. L. (1949): *Northumberland* (London: Robert Hale).

Horsley, P. M. (1971): *Eighteenth Century Newcastle* (Newcastle: Oriel Press).

House, J. W. (1969): *Industrial Britain: The North East* (Newton Abbott: David and Charles).

Howell, R. (1967): *Newcastle Upon Tyne and the Puritan Revolution* (Oxford: Clarendon Press).

Hughes, E. (1952): *North Country Life in the Eighteenth Century: I.—The North East, 1700–1750* (Oxford: Clarendon Press).

Hunter Blair, P. (1970): *The World of Bede* (London: Secker and Warburg).

Iley, W. R. (1974): *Corbridge: Border Village* (Newcastle: Frank Graham).

Jobey, G. (1974): *A Field-Guide to Prehistoric Northumberland: Part 2* (Newcastle: Frank Graham).

Kirby, D. P. (1974): *St. Wilfrid at Hexham* (Newcastle: Oriel Press).

Long, B. (1967): *Castles of Northumberland* (Newcastle: Harold Hill).

McCord, N. (1972): *Northumberland History from the Air* (Newcastle: Frank Graham).

McCord, N., and D. J. Rowe (1971): *Northumberland and Durham: Industry in the Nineteenth Century* (Newcastle: Frank Graham).

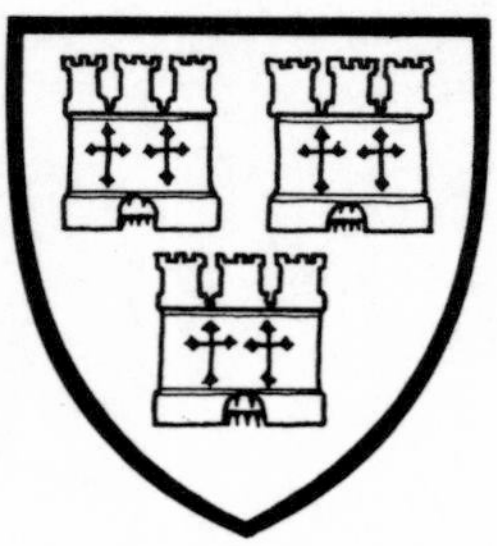

Arms of Newcastle

Mawer, A. (1920): *The Place-Names of Northumberland and Durham* (Cambridge: University Press).
Middlebrook, S. (1950): *Newcastle Upon Tyne: Its Growth and Achievement* (Newcastle: Newcastle Journal).
Middlebrook, S., ed. (1969): *Pictures of Tyneside* (Newcastle: Oriel Press).
Middleton, Sir A. (1918): *Sir Gilbert de Middleton* (Newcastle: privately printed).
Milne, J. M. (1971): *Newspapers of Northumberland and Durham* (Newcastle: Frank Graham).
Newton, R. (1972): *The Northumberland Landscape* (London: Hodder and Stoughton).
Perry, R. (1946): *A Naturalist on Lindisfarne* (London: Lindsay Drummond).
Pevsner, N., and I. A. Richmond (1957): *The Buildings of England: Northumberland* (Harmondsworth: Penguin Books).
Philipson, J., ed. (1969): *Northumberland: National Park Guide 7* (London: H.M.S.O.).
Raistrick, A., and B. Jennings (1965): *A History of Lead Mining in the Pennines* (London: Longmans).
Ramm, H. G., R. W. McDowall, and E. Mercer (1970): *Shielings and Bastles* (London: H.M.S.O.).
Reed, J. (1973): *The Border Ballads* (London: Athlone Press).
Richmond, I. A., ed. (1958): *Roman and Native in North Britain* (Edinburgh: Thomas Nelson).
Robson, D.A. (1966): *A Guide to the Geology of Northumberland and the Borders* (Newcastle: Natural History Society of Northumberland, Durham and Newcastle Upon Tyne).
Rowland, T. H. (1973): *Discovering Northumberland: A handbook of local history* (Newcastle: Frank Graham).
Salway, P. (1965): *The Frontier People of Roman Britain* (Cambridge: University Press).
Sullivan, W. R. (1971): *Blyth in the Eighteenth Century* (Newcastle: Oriel Press).
Tomlinson, W. W. (1897): *Life in Northumberland during the Sixteenth Century* (Newcastle).
Tough, D. L. W. (1928): *The Last Years of a Frontier: A History of the Borders during the Reign of Elizabeth* (Oxford: Clarendon Press).
Trevelyan, G. M. (1934): *The Middle Marches* (London: Longmans).
Watson, G. (1970): *Goodwife Hot and Others: Northumberland's Past as shown in its place-names* (Newcastle: Oriel Press).
Watson, G. (1974): *The Border Reivers* (London: Robert Hale).
Watson, G. (1976): *Northumberland Villages* (London: Robert Hale).
Watts, S. J. (1975): *From Border to Middle Shire: Northumberland 1585–1625* (Leicester: University Press).
White, J. T. (1973): *The Scottish Border and Northumberland* (London: Eyre Methuen).
Wilkes, L., and G. Dodds (1964): *Tyneside Classical* (London: John Murray).
Wilkes, L. (1971): *Tyneside Portraits, studies in art and life* (Newcastle: Frank Graham).
Wilson, D. R. (1967): *Roman Frontiers of Britain* (London: Heinemann).

Arms of Northumberland

Index

Gatehouse at Alnwick Abbey

Old houses, Groat Market, Newcastle, in 1844